HERE COMES THE Sun

STEP UP, SHINE YOUR LIGHT, AND SHARE YOUR BRILLIANCE

COMPILED BY
Misti Wriston

...And 40 Incredible Women Who Said, "Yes!"

Here Comes the Sun
Step Up, Shine Your Light, and Share Your Brilliance
Compiled by Misti Wriston
CampGroundTBD Publishing

Published by CampGroundTBD Publishing, Red Oak, Oklahoma
Copyright ©2022 Misti Wriston
All rights reserved.

No part of this publication may be reproduced, stored in a retrieval system, or transmitted in any form or by any means, electronic, mechanical, photocopying, recording, scanning, or otherwise, except as permitted under Section 107 or 108 of the 1976 United States Copyright Act, without the prior written permission of the Publisher. Requests to the Publisher for permission should be addressed to Permissions Department, CampGroundTBD Publishing at campgroundtbd@gmail.com.

Limit of Liability/Disclaimer of Warranty: While the publisher and author have used their best efforts in preparing this book, they make no representations or warranties with respect to the accuracy or completeness of the contents of this book and specifically disclaim any implied warranties of merchantability or fitness for a particular purpose. No warranty may be created or extended by sales representatives or written sales materials. The advice and strategies contained herein may not be suitable for your situation. You should consult with a professional where appropriate. Neither the publisher nor author shall be liable for any loss of profit or any other commercial damages, including but not limited to special, incidental, consequential, or other damages.

All contributing authors to this anthology have submitted their chapters to an editing process, and have accepted the recommendations of the editors at their own discretion. All authors have approved their chapters prior to publication.

Editor: Cheryl Roberts Oliver

Cover and Interior design: Davis Creative Publishing Partners, CreativePublishingPartners.com

Publisher's Cataloging-in-Publication (Provided by Cassidy Cataloguing Services, Inc.)

Names: Wriston, Misti, compiler.

Title: Here comes the sun : step up, shine your light, and share your brilliance / compiled by Misti Wriston.

Description: Red Oak, Oklahoma : CampGroundTBD Publishing, [2022]

Identifiers: ISBN: 979-8-9863594-0-3 (paperback) | 979-8-9863594-1-0 (ebook) | 979-8-9863594-2-7 (hardback) | LCCN: 2022910222

Subjects: LCSH: Self-actualization (Psychology) in women--Literary collections. | Self-actualization (Psychology) in women--Anecdotes. | Self-esteem in women--Literary collections. | Self-esteem in women--Anecdotes. | Women--Psychology--Literary collections. | Women--Psychology--Anecdotes. | Happiness--Literary collections. | Happiness--Anecdotes. | LCGFT: Self-help publications. | BISAC: SELF-HELP / Motivational & Inspirational. | SELF-HELP / Personal Growth / Happiness. | SELF-HELP / Substance Abuse & Addictions / Alcohol.

Classification: LCC: BF637.S4 W75 2022 | DDC: 158.1/02--dc23

ATTENTION CORPORATIONS, UNIVERSITIES, COLLEGES AND PROFESSIONAL ORGANIZATIONS: Quantity discounts are available on bulk purchases of this book for educational, gift purposes, or as premiums for increasing magazine subscriptions or renewals. Special books or book excerpts can also be created to fit specific needs. For information, please contact CampGroundTBD Publishing at campgroundtbd@gmail.com.

This book is dedicated to
everyone who ever told me yes
and to everyone who ever told me no.
With love and gratitude,
Misti

TABLE OF CONTENTS

Introduction 1
All That Remains 5
Jillian Joy Wallace • The Fire Inside 7
Connie Osterholt • My Baby Girl 13
Sheila Thompson • My Mind and I 19
Shawna Walker • Shadow Work 25
Deborah Driggs • Suffering Quietly 32
Hannah Cecil • After the Rain 39
Barbara Von Schmeling • The Warrior Goddess 44
Jenn Lockhart • The Gift of Desperation 50
Jessica Garza • Actions Speak Louder than Words 56
Trina Ward • The Heart Don't Change 62
Mary Lee Handley • How to Grow a Legacy 68
Roxy Feller • My Dearest Jessica 74
Precious Smith • From the Escape House to the Forever House 80
Kaylee House • Forgiveness and Healing 86
Julia Harriet • The Day After 90
Kenya Evelyn • The Bridge 97
Nataliya Preiss • pHenomenal Life
               From Burnout to Life in Balance 103
Amy Joy • The Power of Perspective 111
Vanessa Tynes-Jass • The First Dark Night 117
Baby Honey • Making Honey 122

Hayley Vanderlois • I Am Stronger 126

Elysia Stobbe • Revelation. 130

Susie Cicchino • A Cup of Abundance. 137

Shay Wood • Plan to Change. 143

Danielle Olbrantz • The Gift of Failure. 148

Laura Jennings • Free Your Unicorn 154

Brenda Long • Sunshine and Lollipops. 160

Lily Quach-Dinh • My Sunshine Connection 166

Mandy Cruz • Dreams in Motion. 172

Martha Moon Gutierrez • Who Rescued Whom?. 178

Ryan Williams • Dancing On My Own 186

Dorothy Stangle • Reflections on Suicide 192

Andrea Marie Yoder • Craving. 198

Julia Parks • Reflections 204

Tammy Thomas • Why I Survived 210

Kristen Salvo • You Can't Pour From an Empty Cup! 216

Heidi Cecil • I'm Just Getting Started. 224

Jen Zoë Hall • Beautifully Broken. 230

Crystal Clenney • Listen Deeper. 237

Devie Richards • Life Beyond Borders 244

Misti Wriston • The Day Dude Had to Die
         and Other Happy Endings 250

Cheryl Roberts Oliver • When Hummingbirds Visit 257

The Afterword 263

Introduction

One of the secrets of life is…there are always more secrets,
especially if we look at things in a new light.

There are times when life is dark, when the light at the end of the tunnel seems unreachable, or artificial. The times we hold an empty cup, knowing it will not pour. Everything we've tried—calories in, calories out, exercise, rise up earlier, budget better, keep a cleaner home, smile, get over it, watch what we say, have more sex, eat fewer carbs, get a flatter stomach and bigger boobs, think happier thoughts, learn to Salute the Sun or Downward Dog, make more money, or do some other thing right—just to make life better. We knew the rules. Trouble is, this shit's not working. (Stay with me, we will address my filthy mouth in a few paragraphs.)

Women used to share the dark and the light: making the perfect pie crust, dropping a baby in a field, managing crippling loss, pain, and disappointment, then with strength and flair displaying our femininity.

We got lost. We lost how to honor being a woman, how to navigate the challenges of women, and, then, how to recover and rise again, better for it all.

We got caught in the dark and thought that made us special. We are not special in our darkness. We are special in our shine and our desire to share.

The sun is always there, even when we cannot see it. There is light no matter how dark it seems. I have lived it and doubted it too. We are not alone. We are *women*.

There are a few important things I want to tell you.

First, I want you to know, right now, on page one: You are *not alone!* There are billions of us, sharing, as has been done for millennia. There is no struggle another woman has not experienced. We are each other! It's unfortunate that we quit speaking about menopause and miscarriage, managing our homes, succeeding with grace, raising children, grieving—just being women.

Second, not everyone in this book has a mouth as filthy as mine. For me, "curse" words provide an emotional outlet. It's OK. Breathe. You do not have to talk like me. There are different voices in this anthology. Find the voice that speaks to you, for you.

Third, there is a joyful, playful, bright life…right on the other side of the most explosive train wreck you've ever experienced. Women with serious bullshit, things no one should ever have to deal with, have found ways to *love life!* Their shit made my shit look festive, and they still managed. It doesn't matter if you can't see it yet, just keep reading. I've read that 90 percent of people don't finish a purchased book. What a waste. Don't be them!

Fourth, what we *know* doesn't mean shit; it is only what we *do now* that fosters change. Knowledge is fluid and ever-changing. *One of the secrets of life is…there are always more secrets, especially if we look at things in a new light.*

Here's the part that may not seem fun. *You* are the only one who can and must decide to step into the light. Decide. *Step up.*

Another wasteful thing is that most people don't fail; they give up! Don't be them!

Introduction

The women who dared to write and place their stories in this anthology did not give up. We invite you to open your heart and learn what they have learned: we are all members of the most beautiful tribe possible, the tribe of women who shine.

Maybe you think you failed, or maybe you've succeeded and thought you should feel differently. I did. I made the money, lost the weight, raised the kids, left the asshole, quit the smoking and drinking, bought the things: fancy car, huge house, long lashes, nice round ass, cute hair. I fucking won at life. I flew first class to eight countries in one year. And I did it by my damn self! As it turned out, I was quite lonely "by my damn self." I was lonely and lost. I was a tribe of one, successful on the outside while protecting my feminine, human insides from the world.

Around the time I "made it," my sweet, unlicensed fifteen-year-old baby boy went sailing through the air in my fancy six-figure convertible at 160 mph. He and his passenger rolled six times, over twelve hundred feet, through barbed wire and on fire, knocking the success tower right out from under me, and the whole thing came tumbling down. All the king's horses and all the king's men could not do shit to help me. I was fucking broken.

I'm not writing this to bring you down. Truthfully, that tragic day saved my family, and I am far from broken now! I was not special in my brokenness. What made me special was my determination to eventually stop my pain. What made me special was finding a tribe of women who chose not to break but to *shine*.

The women who came to my rescue, the light and love they shared, changed me forever. I found unlimited wealth. I found my shine and knew it had to be shared with others. *Shine your light!*

The stories of these women created this book. These beautiful, regular women did irregular things to become whole after learning a lesson. Some could not choose or had to take an unexpected path. We came together to reveal, with our stories, that we all have joyful access to an abundant world.

Are you ready to *share your brilliance?*

Mastering your joy takes work. Self-discipline is hard and yet so simple. Like the simplicity of drinking enough water to stay properly hydrated. Simple enough to frustrate you immensely until it becomes comical and entertaining. Relaxing into the brilliance of women is the hardest, best thing you will ever do for yourself.

My portion of this book grew out of fifty-five years of pain and suffering that ultimately led to a joyful and miraculous life—once I allowed it. I didn't do it in any specific order, with grace or decorum. I didn't even do it well. But I did it! I refused to quit. I refused to waste my life. With discipline, I found love and light and *learned how to hang onto them.*

The more you connect to your tribe, the easier it is to *step up, shine your light, and share your brilliance.* Soak it in. Start now.

Welcome, beautiful Woman, to the sun that shines inside of you.

A woman in your tribe who loves you,

Mistilei

All That Remains

one more step
into that irksome unknown
that taunts and tempts
don't risk it
don't miss this chance
just one step
one decision
once made
alters all that
follows, as
the plague of
"what ifs" crawl inside
you can, you can't
you will, you won't
lifting the foot
putting it down
pulling it back
too risky

too old
too comfortable
you know what you
know so well
your routine
is safe, and yet,
if you don't take
it while you can
that one last chance
to overcome, become
you'll find
too soon is no longer
an option, you've only got
before it's too late.
This is the step
you have to take
to be fully alive for
all that remains.

-Cheryl Roberts

Jillian Joy Wallace

The Fire Inside

It was spring of 2000. I was nineteen years old. I'd just started working at a sales organization about a year before and I was attending a work event in Upstate New York called the Main Event. They had special breakout sessions, and the topic of mine was how to sell high volume. I felt honored to have been asked to present. I was nervous and excited to be speaking alongside a guy I considered (and still do) a legend at the art of salesmanship. He was the kind of salesperson who always did the right thing. I would always be in awe when I saw his numbers come in from a competing office in Maryland. He dwarfed my weekly production numbers with ease.

After a successful day, everyone was feeling great, ready to let their hair down and decompress. The event was being held at an inn that was at the end of a long drive on a country road. It was themed like an old castle. The resort had a dark, sultry bar that turned into a nightclub as the ballrooms emptied of groups. It was the kind of hotel that hosted many work functions like ours. Everyone who was at the seminar that day ended up dancing and drinking in the nightclub that played feel-good music, served bottom-shelf booze, and had dim lighting. We were all so happy, dancing the night away.

I didn't know it at the time, but this scene would be forever burned into my mind. Some moments happen like snapshots, preserved as "the moment right before," or as "the best feeling ever," or some version relived from a magical past life. This moment was a choice I made that is a part now of an ever-altered timeline.

You see, my boss and I worked every day out of his Oldsmobile Bravado SUV. Not just the two of us, but a whole truck of four or five guys and gals. We listened to Bob Seger on cassette tape on the ride home, but only when we had a good day and weren't in discussion about what we could have done better. We had an exceptional team atmosphere, and those days were the foundation of not only my career in sales but also who I've become character-wise.

I loved being part of that era, part of a team that had that special vibe. Although I was young, I quickly learned to take responsibility for my results and be flexible in my approach. We worked hard, and I developed an intense discipline and work ethic. After long days of door-to-door sales were over, and we were satisfied we had served each other and our customers to the best of our ability, my boss would play Seger's *Greatest Hits* album and my favorite song, "The Fire Inside." Seger's familiar voice would fill the truck, and we would sit quietly or sing along softly to ourselves. The familiar classic rock tunes seemed to somehow honor our culture of hard work and dedication. We only listened when we weren't correcting something and because of that, those tunes felt like a job well done.

I remember feeling proud of myself and partying it up with my team in this old castle club. We were in celebration mode—work hard, play hard. We laughed and danced. I felt proud of my speaking job earlier. So many people had showed up to our breakout that the room had gotten hot. People were standing out in the hall taking notes. One girl passed out from the heat. While it was unfortunate that she passed out, I just felt great. I had found my niche as a salesperson, and apparently people wanted to know how I did it. My boss came up to me to tell me he was proud too.

That night, I acknowledged to myself the attraction I had for my boss. It was especially powerful in the context of the day's event and the dimly lit nightclub. I dismissed it; I mean, after all he was my boss. At least I thought I dismissed it, until Bob Seger came on and we both lit up with big smiles. He said, "Come on," and pulled me close to dance. Dancing together to Bob Seger, I felt something I'd never felt. It was a mixture of feeling really proud, joyful, light-hearted, and in love with life itself. I felt electric as the upbeat, old-time rock and roll played and everyone in the bar sang along. Just as the guitar riff started to fade, the lights came up. This was the closing song. We continued to dance awkwardly, not wanting it to be over. It was definitely past when we should have gone to bed if we were to wake up sharp the next day.

As we stood, not wanting to say goodbye, I told him it felt more like Bob Seger's song "The Fire Inside" than it did old-time rock and roll. He laughed, reciting the lyrics "*...the darkness scatters as the lights flash on; they hold one another just a little too long and they move apart and then move on.*" He knew exactly what I meant.

That night I told him that I loved him. I knew we could never be, but I needed to say it. We ended up spending the night together. The next week, the two of us were sitting on my ratty blue couch in the living room of my little apartment in Vermont, and I felt uncomfortable. He was much older than me. We had never been flirty at work, and I was worried we had messed up our relationship. I was self-conscious about the music posters on the walls that made me feel like a kid. I considered myself a bit of a hippie at the time. I had drip candles in bottles, crystals around the house, incense, and a lava lamp. I had carefully sanded and painted the tile in the bathroom and recalked the tub when I moved in. My dad had taught me how to be handy, so I used what I knew to highlight the large farmhouse sink in the kitchen. I painted the walls with grapevine stencils I'd bought at the one Bradlees department store left in the world that was down the street in this one-horse town. It was a young person's apartment, my place.

Back to the *blue-couch conversation*. I was a bit nervous, but I knew I was totally in love with this man. I needed a masculine influence in my life, and he was it. The conversation began with a serious tone, and I knew it would be the kind of conversation that sticks as it unfolds.

"What type of relationship do we want to have? What do we want to accomplish together?" We dove into heavy topics and discussed details at length. We talked totally sober for hours about what we wanted to do and who we wanted to be. We talked about being able to put things down and come back to love. He told me how in his previous relationships they'd said things they didn't mean and how they regretted it because you can't take it back. You can forgive, but forgetting is another story. I agreed. It all felt so healthy. Although it happened fast, I felt there was no other way. I wanted so badly to be a good girlfriend and knew if we could come together, this man would end up being my husband. It felt very different than the start of any relationship I had previously entered.

The blue-couch conversation was one of the reasons we lasted twenty years. I learned everything from how to fix my car to how to be a great salesperson and what I want in a man from two decades with him. There were some hard and painful lessons, some effortless and painless, and some that took a piece of me as their own. Some set the stage for positive precedence, like how we wanted to communicate, and some that set the stage for abuse and other not-so-great things. This conversation shaped our commitment. It was a framework for our relationship that endured the test of time. There are things I wish we had talked about that we didn't, and things that were unspoken. Regardless, the blue-couch conversation was a magical moment in my life. I saw what was coming. I wanted it.

I believe that life-altering magic moments present themselves, and if we see them coming and can get ahead of them, we can decide if we want to let them pass by or feel *the fire inside* and capture every drop of life they contain. Such experiences become placeholders in our memories that, no matter when they come to mind, bring a smile to our faces. My advice: when you can see them coming, don't pass them up.

Jillian Joy Wallace is a sales leader and world traveler. She is passionate about energy and how it shapes our reality in every way. She owns a residential solar energy business and additionally practices energy systems of the body and in the field all around us. As an author, she hopes to be a beacon to electrify, energize, and inspire others to live with intentional magic. She is a dog mom, a feminine force, and a creative coach. The full story of *The Fire Inside* is *The Blue Couch Conversation* and can be found at *www.thebluecouchconversation.com*. Whether you are single and ready to mingle or in a committed relationship, we hope you will enjoy this story in its fullest and create your own blueprint for your very own blue-couch conversation by reading and participating in the ever-evolving multi versions of the sacred blue-couch conversation. So, here's to lovers; may we know them, and may we be them.

www.thebluecouchconversation.com

Connie Osterholt

My Baby Girl

This story is about moving from despair to your soul's destiny. A long time ago, the worst possible thing happened to me. My sweet, beautiful baby girl died because of two gynecologists' decisions that turned out to be the wrong ones, time and again.

In the Netherlands, where I am from and lived at that time, the common belief about childbirth is to have a natural birth even in cases when the baby is breech. Other countries and doctors hold other beliefs and philosophies. If I had been living in the United States, as I do now, I would have seen my baby grow up and be the older sister to my two boys. She was completely healthy and beautiful and died of complications from a breech birth that should have been a cesarean in the first place.

Your child shouldn't die first. It's against the natural order of life's expectations. Parents usually leave their earthly existence first. Children continue as a living legacy, either as a warning or an example, living life as it was meant to be.

My baby, my only daughter, wasn't given that gift.

It all looked so good. The pregnancy was advancing well. I wasn't showing much, and my baby was on the tiny side. When we knew she was breech, they tried to turn her in the right direction, but to no avail. I should have known that she was on her own path already and determined to fulfill her destiny—being as stubborn as her momma.

I created a beautiful little nest at home for her with a hand-decorated family crib in pink and blue with tiny flowers all over. I was a good expectant mother and went diligently to all the checkups with the midwife and the doctors. Two weeks after the due date, I was induced, but for a whole day nothing happened. At night, the hospital was operating on a skeleton crew when I got an uncontrollable storm of contractions, but my body wasn't quite ready for delivery.

There wasn't time to get the C-section operating team ready. The doctors struggled, trying desperately to stop the delivery. But my baby girl was ready to make her entrance. As a breech baby, they couldn't get her out without damaging her brain. After a few short hours, she left Earth. She went to be with what I now know were her angel friends and family.

I was numb, devastated. They were working on her frantically. They wouldn't let me hold her. I couldn't fathom what happened. A lively, healthy, kicking baby girl died. In a frenzy of desperation she was gone, my Stephanie. It was then and still remains incomprehensible.

Here's what I believed and focused on at the time:

- Children should not die before their parents.
- It's unnatural to have this reversed.
- If only I would have been more assertive and asked for a c-section.
- I did not protect my little girl.
- I did not take care of her.
- If only I had lived in America, where breech babies are given a C-section, I would have had a healthy baby.

I was so angry at myself for not speaking up; at my husband; at the doctors, midwife, and nurses for making the mistakes they did. They should have known better; they didn't do their job. I was angry at God for letting an innocent baby die. How could he? For no good reason. God is cruel. God does not exist.

When I came home with empty arms, my mother and sister-in-law had dismantled the baby room and stowed everything that I so lovingly put together for my girl. It was like everybody denied her existence, wanted to forget her. My husband didn't want to talk about what happened. I could not register her name with city hall because she died the same day. I remember her living inside of me for more than nine months, my sweet girl. My Stephanie.

My friends either avoided me or said, "You are young, you'll get another baby." Like she did not count. Or was replaceable. Instead of comforting me, it made me feel all alone and so sad. My more advanced friends were hinting at what the gift or lesson was in all of this. I couldn't even hear it. Why would my baby girl have to die in order to give me a lesson? I would have given my own life in a heartbeat if it could have saved her.

I cried and cried and cried some more. I'll never forget her funeral, the tiny white coffin, the pink baby roses, and the music. "Für Elise"—for years and years after, I teared up when hearing this piece. I felt helpless, angry, out of control, sad, alone, frustrated.

I came to understand that society only allows you to mourn in public for so long. It's about six weeks. After that you need to be strong, courageous, and move on. At least in my country. Move on, get pregnant, have a new family. Probably all very well meant, but I couldn't find my way around it. I complied, put on a mask, a mask of saying and behaving like I was fine. On the inside, though, I was still crying.

Few people were ready to talk about my loss, the hurt, the pain. Most avoided the topic. I understood where they were coming from. They simply did not know what to say or do. But it felt as if they were not understanding me, like no one felt or wanted to acknowledge my loss. My life, my empty world.

I was declared physically healthy again pretty soon, but nobody cared for my emotional and spiritual health. My emotions were in a constant turmoil, churning from the anger and frustration. My spirit was squashed, depressed, dark. My light was dimmed, or maybe it had died with my baby girl.

Being a responsible adult, I knew I couldn't go on like this. In my mind I was willing to move on, I just didn't know how. My heart and soul were aching, and I didn't know how to change that. I learned to live with what happened. It became part of how I showed up—reserved and guarded. Life was divided between what was going on in front of my mask and what happened behind it. I suppressed the hurt and pain in order to function in daily life. Not really happy, not really unhappy, living in neutral.

After ten tears of living like this, I began to question the validity of doing so. I felt a glimmer of hope that maybe, just maybe, there was more to life than I was experiencing. I started looking for books, courses, people with similar experiences. I was curious and researched the psychology of it all, which was one of my interests from the past.

I have read books and been to many personal development seminars, both emotional and spiritual, and I found people willing to help me through, people who were kind and compassionate enough to let me talk and cry. They offered their shoulders to cry on and loved me through the process of rediscovering meaning and purpose.

I learned so much about myself, my heart, my soul, my mission and purpose in life. I learned the power of having beliefs that support you, choosing emotions that are good, focusing on loving *what is*, and always seeing possibilities.

I learned to love me and forgive myself, and also to forgive everyone involved with my daughter's birth. I learned to forgive God. I saw the possibility of change—changing my life and also changing the lives of people who'd endured grief themselves.

I was finally able to understand that my beautiful baby girl had a purpose to her little life. I am so grateful for her, and I know she is with me and around me all the time. Her purpose was and still is to help me understand my purpose in life, to be courageous, compassionate, loving, caring, and most of all understanding of complex human nature. To comprehend how people process whatever they are going through. To help them see the possibility of changing. To help them access their own emotional and spiritual resources. To be kind, loving, and compassionate, and to be willing to make a difference in the lives of the people I came across. To be the best I can be and to be a role model of what is possible.

I became a speaker, author, and my own version of a person helping people shape their lives to be better and more fulfilled. A coach, if you will.

I am not forgetting what happened in my life, but I am growing with all that is, the good and the bad. I have learned to be wise and understanding. I have learned to listen in such a way that I can detect patterns in the subconscious mind that activate a response to a trigger, a response that is usually outdated and not the best choice for your situation.

I have become a consummate translator of what communication and experience can really mean for you, and how you can become even better as you travel on your path toward growth and happiness. There is always a way.

With a PhD in Psychoneurology, Connie Osterholt has focused her career on understanding behaviors, personalities, and mindsets so she can help individuals, teams, and businesses achieve more success and fulfillment. Her starting point is to recognize patterns that work and patterns that are ready for an upgrade. She is skilled in training, teaching, communications, leadership, and coaching businesses, teams, and individuals. Knowing that clarity is power, she applies her knowledge and experience to making difficult concepts more easily understood and to diversifying communication based on an individual's personalized and behavioral preferences. She earned a bachelor's degree in physical education at The Hague University and excelled on a national level in field hockey and badminton, then turned to the study of movement performance. Dean of Beurin University Woodland Hills, California, from August 1997 to the present, she is also engaged at Robbins Research International in San Diego. She has performed in support of Tony Robbins at his events and as a speaker, Master Platinum Coach, and Master/Lead Trainer.

www.drconnieonline.com
www.facebook.com/connie.osterholtphd
drconnieosterholt@gmail.com

Sheila Thompson

My Mind and I

A woman goes through many changes, many versions of herself, to find her most authentic being. We are all chasing who we truly are.

My story begins in 1967 in a small, two-bedroom house in the sweltering Oklahoma heat. It was August, and my mother labored with me for three days before I decided to be born. I was their first child and the first grandchild. I had a picture-perfect, small-town America upbringing, except, about the time I began to crawl, we discovered I was hyperactive. My mind and body raced at a speed that was hard to keep up with. My mom cleaned up one mess and bounced another toddler on her hip while I made another mess. It was a circus. I was the circus! Which could be comical except it was my life. It didn't take long for my parents to begin researching my symptoms, and they found a specialist in Texas who could help me.

We went to Dallas for glucose tolerance tests. One particular day of testing, we ventured out of the hospital for a break. As we walked, I saw a sweet shop. We went inside and before anyone realized, I had gobbled down a cookie. I was supposed to be fasting for the tests. Mortified, we raced back to the doctor's office, and he embraced the opportunity to see what this did to the rest of the day's tests. We watched my levels go off the top of the page. Sugar was my enemy. Except that it was my best friend. My little body craved sugar in a very real and serious way. I was prescribed

Ritalin. It helped me cope as a child, but having to rely on a pill made me feel different.

My adolescence and early adulthood years were all about me chasing myself. Lost, unsure, I was always told I was "too much" and "out of control." I lived up to those words! I believed them. I also didn't know how to be different. I wanted so badly to have control over myself, my racing thoughts. Insecurities and self-doubt seemed to be the only things I could hold onto.

Awkward teen years turned into awkward young adult years. The only tool I had in my tool kit was medication. I medicated myself through twenty-five years of my life with everyone who knew and loved me as a witness. My mistakes created a hole too deep to climb out of. I failed my child, my parents, and myself, and while I could have stayed dug in, this story is about a *comeback girl.*

The next version of my life began in February 2012, when, at the same moment, I both lost and found myself. I was lying on a cold cement floor, locked behind bars, with no idea how or why I was there. It occurred to me that God loved me enough to love me hard, and that it was time I took control of myself. I could no longer medicate my life away.

The uphill climb out of a life gone astray takes courage. Big, wild, brave courage. I was at my lowest point without my coping tool. My toolbelt was empty and I was raw inside. Most people in my life looked at me as if I were a lost cause, hanging off the wagon, ready to jump at any moment. The only card I had left to play was to show them. Defiant, determined, I swore I would show them I could do it, that I could overcome!

Making a decision to change is one thing. The changes that come next are an entirely different thing. I spent six more years being miserable, angry, and lost, *but I was clean.* Misery actually *doesn't* love company. I knew I wasn't fun to be around, not at work or in family situations. I was the chameleon hiding in a prickly-pear cactus of my own making, and it didn't take much to ruin an entire day. I was as fragile as I had ever been, *but I was clean.* I was lost at every holiday. I either wasn't in the stories told at the table or I didn't remember them. I decided I just wasn't suitable for life, or life wasn't suitable for me. I had no mark to leave on this earth. The outlook was bleak. *Clean me wasn't the person I thought she would be.*

Then one day, by happenstance, a woman I admired, Jill Donovan, Owner of Rustic Cuff, posed a question and asked for written responses: "What would you do if you knew you wouldn't fail? If you took failure out of the equation, what might you accomplish?"

That was the rope I used to pull myself out of the hole. I handwrote a letter describing exactly what I would do if I knew I wouldn't fail and sent it to the woman who had posed the question. She was a local celebrity, owner of a fashion business. One day my phone rang at work. I didn't recognize the number, so I didn't answer. The call came through a second time. I answered and heard the voice of the woman to whom I'd written the letter.

She said, "Since you included your phone number, I decided to call you." The note that I wrote, and then the call, ignited a creative revolution in my life. I began thinking outside myself and found a more positive place to heal myself, changing my thinking from a negative "can't do" mindset to a positive "try it" approach.

The next big step I took toward rebuilding myself was a physical challenge. My son had recently graduated from the Fire Academy and was becoming a firefighter in one of the best departments in the nation. Part of the guilt and shame of my life had been that I was not the best parent, but somehow this beautiful son of mine excelled at everything he tried. He stood tall in the face of adversity, even when it was his parent. Our fire department offers a citizens academy, and I signed up. I wanted to learn and see what my son would be facing in his new role. I had no idea what I was in for.

Within weeks, I was learning how to suit up in gear, put out fires, give commands on the radio, rappel out of an eight-story building, and administer CPR on dummies as well as put in an IV. This was by far the most empowering thing I have ever done. I was rebuilding myself with strength and confidence.

Once I completed the course, I bought myself work boots and overalls, and I began tackling chores at home: trimming trees, doing yardwork, attending to housework that needed done for years. I felt *unstoppable*. Once again, I felt empowered.

In the winter of 2019 I began painting the interior walls in my house. I painted every single wall in my house by myself. As I painted, the thought came to me that I should maybe try to repurpose some of my furniture. I researched and began buying paints to give my home and furnishings a new look. One Saturday my mom handed me a picture and said, "Look what this girl is doing with furniture." I jumped on it.

My painting journey that began with painting signs and repurposing furniture for home decor is now a thriving business of canvas art, crafty inventions, and original works. Creativity, paint, and art gave me a life, showed me the way home. I found the person I had been searching for all along. All my life I felt like a circle trying to fit into a square peg. It took me fifty years to find where I belonged. There were many times along the journey when giving up would have been much easier. I was the last hope for myself. I did not give up.

The messages I give myself are different now. As women, we are so very hard on ourselves. I allow myself to recognize the different women I hold inside. I acknowledge them and how they all play a part in the whole version of who I am. I was stuck in teenager mode for too many years.

I can see that now. I am now able to recognize the grandmother in me, the mom and caretaker, the artistic girl and creative child, the critic, the firecracker. Once I started to notice how I react and respond to people, and through which version of myself, I was able to adapt and control my reactions and responses. When the message comes in as "I can't do this;" I stop, breathe, and respond from a version of myself that says, "Yes, you can." By changing the messages I was thinking, I was able to use the most powerful tool I have—my mind. My mind and I learned to love all the bits and pieces of this human work of art.

My message is simple. *Do it until it feels right.* I am living proof it works.

The girl on a cement floor, lost and forlorn, now makes art and vibrantly colors her own world. The hands that shook from fear now paint patterns and create magic on canvas. I work two jobs and have a home I love, dogs I adore, and grandbabies who hang the moon in my world. I feel loved in my tribe and, above all else, I can say today I am proud of who I have become. I love fiercely. I found my world. So can you.

This chapter is dedicated to my dad, who has loved me and believes in me without condition or reason. In the ugly moments and in the beautiful moments. My one goal in life is to make him proud. I hope my life has come full circle enough for his heart to be filled with pride at the path I've created. Standing tall, Dad!

Sheila Thompson is an intuitive abstract artist living in Oklahoma City, Oklahoma. Her intense curiosity and soul-guided creativity led her to canvas art. Each canvas she creates is born from the rhythm of the music that fills the air and the beauty of nature around her, both of which have been her guides on her path of self-awareness. Observing her mom create art and interact with a group of artists every week for over forty years gave Sheila a firm foundation on which to build. The tools were there all along, but it wasn't until she was in her fifties that Sheila picked up a brush and paints to set out on a new journey. She lives with her two rescue pups, Turbo and Wookie. She has an adult son who is a firefighter, a beautiful daughter-in-law who is a schoolteacher, and three little grandchildren who bring light to her world. By day, Sheila works in the auto repair industry and cleans homes for the elderly on weekends. By night, and in all the spare moments in between, her fingers are covered in paint as she sits on the floor or stands in front of an easel, madly creating and enjoying life.

https://www.facebook.com/profile.php?id=100063552042319

Shawna Walker

Shadow Work

"We can easily forgive a child who is afraid of the dark; the real tragedy of life is when we are afraid of the light."
— Author Unknown

Do you ever wonder why you keep attracting the same type of people and circumstances into your life? Are you tired of always feeling stuck or wondering "why me?" I've wondered, felt, and asked all these things. I've dwelled on the hurts I experienced from others' words and/or hands, literally replaying the moments again and again in my head. I kept feeling all of the emotions that were involved—hurt, shame, sadness, anger, abandonment. I was alone and literally stuck in my past.

Guess what happened? All those circling thoughts and instant replays didn't change a thing. But I couldn't stop the churning. It was inside. It began to manifest into physical ailments. I would release it by lashing out at someone, starting an argument. I knew this repetitive cycle had to stop! I also knew that emotions always come out, one way or another.

I used Shadow Work to uncover my own darkness. It changed my life.

What Is Shadow Work?

It's hard, frustrating, and scary. It's taking the time to delve beyond habitual thoughts and feelings, actions and reactions. This work gets *behind* what is actually happening.

Do you get so caught up in the moment that you just have to have your say with the other person, but you never stop to consider that the cause of your reactions may not have anything to do with them at all? They are just triggering something that you are holding onto. Something you may not even remember is there. Shadow Work is about learning to re-parent yourself and heal your inner child. Shadow Work is the most meaningful gift you can give yourself.

Here's how it works for me. There are certain phrases or words that trigger me. In the past I would have become defensive. Began to point out all of the other person's faults. Basically, I would attempt to deflect all the attention away from my own mistakes instead of listening and taking the time to truly look at myself and my part in the situation.

Now when someone says something that hits my trigger, I take a moment. I breathe. I take another moment to consider the words they have said. Then I dive into my subconscious and find where that trigger originated. It's like being an explorer into my past, and I go back as far as I can remember.

I haven't always been able to do it. And I'm not about to say that I have "mastered" the process. What I will say is that when I can calm myself and stay focused, I recognize that I'm *responding from pain in my past.*

These triggers need to be found. They need to be uncovered and examined. I finally decided to stop wasting my energy running from the pain, and now I stop to feel it. *Through the pain is truly the way out of the pain.*

So how does it work? What needs to be done?

Decide You Are Ready

This is the first and most important step in Shadow Work.

- Think about a person in your life who pushes your buttons.
- Make a list of the things about them that bother you.
- Give it some time, then when you're ready, look at the list again. Think about yourself this time and not them. Anything look familiar?

Be completely honest with yourself. This person is just a mirror of you. Are you judging someone for being rude? I guarantee if you stop and pay attention to your actions and words, you will find your rudeness. Don't judge it. Identify it and study it. Continually ask yourself questions. How was I rude? Why was I rude to that person? Is this a pattern? Who did I learn it from? All of these questions will lead to more questions. And if you run out of questions, you can always ask "why?"

Feel the Emotions

The next step is to allow yourself to feel the emotions the trigger has caused. Allow yourself to cry if you're sad. Find a safe way to express the anger if you're angry. Allow yourself to feel these things. Do it until you're exhausted. Then rest. Breathe. And remember, you may do this step a number of times before you eventually find the core of these emotions and reactions.

I assure you, based on my personal experiences, it is more than worth the effort. I have been through the first and second steps more times than I care to admit. I will again. But now I know it is just a sign that there is still something about myself that I need to discover. I can also tell you that I am worth that effort. And so are you!

Delve Into Your Past

This next step can be quite intense, depending on your personal journey. You are going to delve into your past and dig up stagnant memories that your conscious mind has been attempting to shield from you.

Ask yourself questions about the trigger. Start by identifying how you felt when the trigger happened. Where is this feeling really coming from? Sit with the emotions. Notice the changes in your body while you consider the trigger. Where do you feel it most? Then talk to your emotions. They are here to teach you. Spend some time asking them questions. Why am I feeling this way now? If it is because someone said or did something specific, examine it. Do this step without judgement or blame. Remember, that person is a mirror for you. Every person who comes into your life is a mirror for you. Yes, even that ex who still drives you crazy with the thoughts that are stuck in your head was in your life to teach you something. You just have to be brave enough to listen.

Also begin to notice where you are being judgmental of someone else. If you are only observing the behavior, it most likely is *not* a part of your Shadow. If you are instead judging that person for their actions or words, you can be assured it lies in you somewhere, somehow. The judgement we project onto others actually reflects qualities we possess in ourselves but deny.

You Are the Judge and Jury

How often do you ignore your feelings or bury them with distractions and addictions? Too much work, television, food, alcohol, drugs, Facebook...well, you know. All the things that you do instead of unburying the emotions and working through them. When you distract yourself from your emotions, the negative feelings simply wait and grow. You tend to go down that proverbial rabbit hole of "what if," "why me," and "I'm better than them." That's when you may begin to judge yourself and your actions, becoming harder and harder on yourself than you were before.

Instead, *name the judgements*. Don't ignore or explain them away. Learn from them and move past them so you can enjoy some peace in your life.

Take a break

When I first discovered Shadow Work, I went at it hard! I experienced many nights when I felt like my entire soul was purging the tears and anger, the resentment and fear. Small little glimpses would begin to emerge, giving me something else to examine. I was committed to the process, though. I still am. But I also give myself permission to take a break, albeit never a very long one.

If you are triggered and don't have the time or motivation to work on it in the moment, write it down so you can come back to it. Trust me, it will just continue to appear. If the Universe has something to teach you and you aren't paying attention, something will show up to trigger you. That's OK if it does. Learn from it, use it.

Your Own True Voice

I'm going to talk about those little voices that speak to us, especially when something or someone triggers us. Part of this process is learning to discern which voice is the genuine one. Most of the voices we hear come from childhood, our parents, or maybe teachers and others in authority. They can be ancestral or cultural, ingrained or learned.

During Shadow Work, you are on the hunt for *your own true voice*. Not the ones that you have picked up along the way as defense mechanisms. This doesn't mean you allow yourself to become a pushover. In Shadow Work, look for that balance between standing firm in your boundaries and allowing others to walk all over you. Rid yourself of reactions that no longer serve you.

There Are No Shadows Without Light

Some days it is the sun that casts shadows, the days that are bright with beautiful colors. Others are dark and gloomy. And still others are a mix of the two. Going through any type of healing process and emerging on the other side doesn't mean that every day will be perfect or even close to it. Something will always come up to test your resolve and your commitment to yourself. Looking at your childhood can be difficult, overwhelming work. Keep a journal to show all the progress you have made. Look for repeating patterns that you might not otherwise notice as well as the habitual behaviors you don't even think about.

Shadow Work will touch all aspects of your life. It will be physical, emotional, mental, and soul work. It is the only work that heals and shines a light on the parts of yourself you hide. Shine the light. Do the Shadow Work. You owe it to yourself.

Shawna Walker grew up in Edmond, Oklahoma, graduated high school in the late eighties, and immediately began working in the Early Childhood field. She's given birth to three of the most amazing men on this planet. She's been married twice but is now happily single and living her best possible life. When Shawna's youngest moved out, she decided to purchase a vehicle and go wherever she wanted, whenever she wanted. She's slept on the beach, in an alley, and stayed with many friends along the way. She's explored cemeteries and abandoned houses. Since putting in the time doing her Shadow Work, Shawna's been able to just enjoy the little things that life has to offer. She has been amazingly blessed, and she's honored to work on this project—which has inspired her to write more! She's finally looking forward to all the new chapters this life has for her.

www.facebook.com/Roadside-Revelations-111320978023586/

Deborah Driggs

Suffering Quietly

Did you know that women are taken down quicker and faster by alcohol than men are? Women's bodies absorb alcohol much faster than men's bodies, and women are more at risk for physical damage caused by alcohol.

It was incredibly difficult to label myself an alcoholic, let alone a person with an addiction. I just could not surrender to the knowledge that I had to stop drinking to heal. Getting sober was the hardest thing I have ever done, harder even than the twelve-hour extreme adventure races I used to do!

I knew from an early age that I had a problem; I just wasn't sure what it was. I was angry and rebellious in my teens. By the age of eighteen, I had been arrested twice and put in jail. I still would not surrender to the idea that alcohol was making my life worse. I white-knuckled for years, holding on for dear life.

I did not always drink, and I could go days or months without alcohol, so I was somewhat baffled when I finally decided to surrender once and for all. Many people would tell me, "Deb, you are not an alcoholic," and that would confuse me even more. I knew I drank too much. Deep down I knew the truth. I was suffering quietly, alone, afraid that if I said I had a problem, everything would change. I was definitely in a dark place.

In my twenties I thought I was just having fun. I was the life of the party, the one who made people laugh. I was the girl you called if you wanted to go out and have fun. Anything could happen. I did crazy stuff and lost my moral compass. My friends had to remind me of the things we did the night before because I blacked out and couldn't remember. Deep down it felt dark, and there was nothing laughable about it. I never felt good about blacking out, but that is where alcohol took me. It wasn't about how much I drank; I always had a hard time remembering what happened the night before. The details were foggy.

Living a lie is lonely. I was successful and well liked, while on the inside my soul was dying. I couldn't believe other people could drink and remember the night before when I could not. I knew I was getting progressively worse.

My drinking mellowed in my thirties, but my suffering increased. The darkness got worse. I was married and had three children, which reduced the amount of drinking, and when I did drink, I got sick. I was still living a lie. On the outside I had a beautiful husband and three beautiful babies. On the inside I was in so much emotional pain. No matter what I tried, the pain would not stop. I am an extremist, so I started training like crazy, four to six hours a day. During my adventure racing days, great endorphins were getting released. My suffering was so bad that not even adventure racing and being in the best shape of my life could make me feel better. This was not the cure.

On the outside, everything looked good, but *this was an inside job*. The emotional healing that I needed was nowhere in reach. It also did not help that I suffered with postpartum depression after my third baby. I had three babies back-to-back, which took a huge toll on my body. I was severely depressed and tired. I was beating myself up instead of giving myself love and care. I thought something was definitely wrong with me. I remember when Brooke Shields revealed that she suffered from postpartum and took medication and then Tom Cruise bashed her on national TV for taking a pill—and I kept quiet!

In my forties I hit rock bottom. *I was suffering—quietly.* The progression of this horrible addiction brought me to my knees. I had no clue what was making me hurt this bad. I did not know yet that I suffered from trauma and alcoholism. Bad combo. So I did the worst thing possible and attempted to end it—once and for all. My relationship with alcohol was so bad I had a nervous breakdown, and in a moment of impulsive decision-making, when I was overwhelmed with darkness and soul sickness, I took a bottle of pills and chased them down with vodka.

I ended up in a lockdown situation. For the next two months I had to learn how to walk again—not literally, but having had my life saved, I had to walk out of the darkness. I honestly knew nothing about recovery, so I learned everything I could, especially how things can come to a head if you do not deal with issues early on. I didn't know about the disease of alcoholism or, more importantly, how it affects women. So I learned.

I spent months in rehab learning about addiction. While I was in rehab I thought, "Well, this isn't that bad." Denial at its finest. Resistance at its finest. The sickness was there, but my ego would not let go. I left rehab thinking, "I got this," which was a huge mistake.

I went back into the dark and spent years drinking, slowly sliding down the rabbit hole. Addiction can be a fast killer or a slow killer. For me it was a slow kill. Here is the good news. I now knew that when I drank, it wasn't going to be good, so drinking was not fun anymore.

In my fifties, still looking for a solution, I abandoned research and took up deep soul searching. I would do whatever I had to do to get out of the dark. I mean, how does this actress/model and successful businesswoman end up on a soul-searching mission? How does that happen when on the outside it looked as if I had everything? And yes, I had more than enough. I had hit most of my goals—financial goals, business goals, creative goals—but I was still suffering.

Then it finally hit me!

One day when I finally confided in someone that I was suffering, they said to me, "Wow, really? You always look as though you have it all together!"

Drop a piano on my head! I wondered how many other people were like me, suffering quietly. I went on a mission. I started reading every book on trauma and healing. I checked into a rehab facility to work on trauma. When I left that rehab, I realized there was no follow-up program for what I wanted to do. There are a lot of amazing twelve-step programs, but I wanted to do more intensive work.

I woke up at 2:00 a.m. in November 2020 with the decision to create a ninety-day program. I enrolled in a life coaching program (I have done a few now) and started writing a weekly blog geared toward people like me who are quietly suffering. I am no longer in the darkness, although sometimes in the middle of the night I still feel fearful and anxious.

Today I dance with that fear and anxiety. It does not take me down or isolate me. I work with it. I stay sober from the neck up one day at a time. I write every day. I coach every day. I work with people with addiction. What a gift!

Removing everything from my life that did not serve me was a huge step. Addiction comes in many forms: alcohol, drugs, pills, shopping, sex, food, traveling, gambling. You get it. So I removed all of it. When I had my 2:00 a.m. wake-up call, I outlined on two white boards what this healing would look like. At this point in my soul-searching endeavor, I had done yoga retreats, pranic healing, energy cleansing, life coaching with some-of-the-best-in-the-world life coaches, silence retreats, meditation retreats, Happiness Is a Way of Life retreats, and even the 75 Hard mental toughness program! As I was writing on my whiteboards, I kept thinking, "Deb, you have spent time, money, and energy doing all these seminars and retreats! *Do your own!*" And so I did.

I wrote on one whiteboard everything I was removing for ninety days and on the other whiteboard everything I was giving myself. It was like a diet for the soul. Time to kill off bad eating habits and start eating tasty, healthy, nutritious food. Knowing it is never good to take something away without giving something in return, I thought about how our brains heal by holding good thoughts, not just by removing bad ones. It is a give-and-take.

Using this give-and-take model, I created Deb's Den, a safe space to heal. This time I was committed to healing. I stopped traveling and every other negative distraction, including the way I used social media. I changed completely. I got to work. Let the soul cleansing begin!

I still felt resistance to this change. Some days I was on my knees, ready to give up! My mind kept saying, "Get on a plane and go to Cabo. Drink margaritas and eat chips and guacamole." My old habits really wanted to take me down, but I stuck to my ninety-day program. When I completed my ninety days, I kept going, because by then the pain had lessened, and I liked the results.

I am in recovery. It is a daily practice to keep staying positive. I pray, meditate, drink water, do yoga, work, write, read, eat healthfully, and spend time with loved ones. Most importantly, I am of service.

Looking at my part in every situation has been the biggest gift. Obviously, with years of drinking (I started very young), I owed a lot of amends. What a beautiful gift to be able to own my part in every situation. Let me be very clear: today I do not blame anything on my drinking, as I had done for years. Every day, I have a choice to pick up a drink or not. What I do know is nothing good will come to me if I do. I also know I cannot be an example to the people I truly want to help if I start again. My greatest realization was that I get way more out of helping and coaching than any drink ever gave me.

This chapter is about getting a glimpse of what life can actually look like without an addiction tugging at you. This is the solar eclipse of change, an opening for newly formed self-care habits. It is a beautiful surrender into a magical way of thinking, a surrender made with guidance and love, especially self-love. It is about learning to love ourselves first, healing ourselves first, and learning how to be alone with our feelings and thoughts. I don't know about you, but I never learned these skills growing up. These skills need to be taught and shared, learned and practiced.

Emotional education is where it is at today. Mental illness is real and affecting too many to count. It is time to shift the paradigm and break historical trauma stories passed down generation after generation. I get to break the pattern in my gene pool. What a gift! I mean generations of traumas that I wasn't even a part of but are lying dormant in my nervous system. Interesting, right? Healing my past genetic traumas is going to heal future generations. We get to stop these patterns.

I have a team of coaches, mentors, healers, and holistic doctors to help keep me in check. I cannot and will not do this alone. When I am suffering quietly, isolation feels normal. It is not normal. If you find yourself isolating and wanting to be alone more and more, please check in with someone about that. Remember, the ego wants to take over.

This chapter is not for everyone, but I was called to write to those who suffer like I did. Put your hands on your heart and let the Universe do its magic. You and I are not alone. We never were. Guidance and healing are available; we just need to tap into them!

I want to thank all the women who have guided me on my journey to sobriety. Many have shown me how to live gracefully. I will be forever grateful for those beautiful, inspiring women. They save my ass every day and keep my spirit shining in the sunlight!

Deborah Driggs is on a healing path. Known for her acting roles in *Night Rhythms*, *Total Exposure*, and *Neon Bleed*, she has also been a *Playboy* centerfold and cover girl, a member of the Screen Actors Guild, and a top-rated insurance industry professional. Deborah has overcome a number of challenges by being willing to take risks and maintain a positive attitude. Pursuing her interest in dance, Deborah won a spot on the US Football League cheerleading squad and joined a professional dance company touring Japan. When she returned to Los Angeles, she began her modeling career and auditioned for *Playboy*. After posing as a centerfold, she was invited to grace the cover of the March and April 1990 issues of *Playboy*—the leading men's magazine in the world at the time—which led to opportunities as a VJ (video jockey) for the Playboy Channel's *Hot Rocks* show and appearances in several rock videos. Dedicated to helping women break through negative self-talk and take on any challenge, Deborah knows the difference it can make to have a helping hand when one needs it the most. Her response to internal struggles is, "If there is a struggle, then there is a problem, and in that problem there is a beautiful, simple solution for complicated souls!"

www.deborahdriggs.com
deborah@deborahdriggs.com
www.imdb.com/name/nm0237910/ (Deborah Driggs—IMDb)

Hannah Cecil

After the Rain

I'm Hannah, and I am sixteen years old. When I was younger I dreamed of getting older, doing the things adults do. I didn't know what growing up involved, but I knew I wanted to start my growing-up journey early.

My family had issues, as most do. Mine involved drug addicts and abusers. I love my family, of course. My mom was a drinker. She would wobble to my room and yell and ground me for any reason she could find. My brother, sister, and father tried to protect me, but my father left when I was eleven, then my siblings grew up and left home. Not long after, I started getting into a lot of trouble.

I felt alone. Mostly I was angry. I had a friend who made me feel less alone, but to keep her friendship, I ended up doing whatever she wanted, which was drugs and meeting boys. I wanted to feel *something* and have fun. I went along with everything she wanted to do. We would sneak out and run away. I did whatever I could to feel better, and it ended up taking three years of my life.

During those three years, I failed most of my classes. I didn't care what happened to me. I didn't care about my grades. It was all about having fun. I hated going home to a toxic household that made me want to escape even more. The constant yelling, chaos, and bad decisions were consuming me. I was at my limit.

I stopped being friends with that girl, so I was alone again. By this time, I knew I had to get better or else risk being put somewhere I didn't want to be. So I worked on myself. It wasn't easy. I tried exercising and listening to a lot of music. That helped, but it wasn't enough.

I decided to start dating. It wasn't a great idea. I couldn't find the right person. I cried a lot. Actually, I just wasn't healthy enough for a relationship. I didn't have space for anyone else because I despised everything about myself. I hated my waist, boobs, teeth, how tall I was, and even my hair. I needed to learn to love me. I thought I'd love myself more if I lost weight, so I stopped eating. I dropped weight fast and soon found myself unable to eat.

My mother was worried and gave me medical marijuana to fix it. It helped me feel better. But it wasn't enough. I ended up needing it every time I was going to eat or go out or do anything. I did get healthy again, although I was dependent on the escape it gave me for my anxiety. I tried new things. I felt better. But this was during the summer.

School was a whole new chapter. My first year of high school was terrifying. I didn't know where I fit in. I struggled a lot. I was trying new hairstyles almost every other week, crazy new outfits, and anything else to make myself look different. I still had this hole in me. I tried to fill it by being busy, but I still felt empty. So I went looking for a partner or friend.

I met this guy, and I thought I liked him. But soon I realized he was unhealthy, unkind, and controlling. Which wasn't good for me. He broke up with me and accused me of cheating when he had been cheating on me for months. I became very depressed. I had been cutting off and on. No one knew what to do. There really wasn't anything anyone could have done.

Here's what I learned: *No one can help if you don't want help.* And I didn't. I didn't need someone to hold my hand. No one ever had before, so why would I need it now? I was wrong. Everyone needs someone. At least a hug. I wish I had known that then. Instead I pushed everyone away and ignored them.

Finally, I got a therapist and was diagnosed with BPD—Borderline Personality Disorder—severe depression, and anxiety. I did some research and discovered some of the reasons I felt the way I did—empty, sad, angry, and so alone. I also learned why I did things impulsively and how to stop. I knew I had to, or my future would be empty.

Up to that time, I didn't even think about or want a future, if you know what I mean. But I told myself I wouldn't be in that house forever and that it was time to start focusing on my future. I began my second semester of high school, and it was a little better. I wasn't dating anyone, but that wasn't bad. Nadine and Janice were my best friends. I don't remember much from my second semester of freshman year. It's all a blur. After that semester, I shifted gladly into summer because I was exhausted from the mental stress I got from school and home.

I met this guy named Mason. He came over every night after he got off work, and we would talk and watch movies. Apparently he lost interest, because he stopped responding or would ghost me, taking hours or days to answer. I felt used and angry. I still had Nadine and Janice, and they helped fill my time.

I felt stuck again as I struggled to make decisions and take action, and I started sneaking out to do things I shouldn't be doing. To punish . . . who was I punishing?

Another thing I learned: *You have to want to get better to get better.* I was back in the trap of not wanting to be or get better. Life sucked. I figured out I was going through manic-depressive episodes and would for the rest of my life. I learned how to cope and calm myself. I got my medical card to help with my sleep problems, anxiety, and eating problems, along with everything else.

I didn't know what I wanted. I isolated myself and fell back into doing it alone again. I didn't want to do it alone. I wanted help but didn't know how to ask for it, where to look for it.

I learned: *It's OK to need help.* I picked up the pieces and got busy. I met someone who was really good for me, kept me on track. A real best friend who helped me find a reason to keep going and keep getting better. We ended up getting together.

I got a job, which I still have, and my life is on track now. I'm getting my driver's license in a few months. I'm planning on moving. I just need to take care of and care about myself. I need to figure out what kind of future I want, and then believe in it.

It's really hard finding the right mindset. I still struggle, and it can be rough. Knowing nothing is forever helps me get through each day. The good comes with the bad. Change is possible.

In fact, my mother pulled herself out of the rut she was in and is now a better person. She still tends to fall back into her old patterns, but no one is perfect. As for my father, he lives about forty-five minutes away. We don't really talk much, even though I go there twice a month.

What really makes me wonder is how they can be so disinterested in me or my life. I tell myself it's okay, that they're just living their lives. Just like I'm trying to do.

Now I'm sixteen, and for the first time I feel like I have a bright future. To envision that future, I learned that what I'm going through *doesn't define me*. That I can get through it. I have to keep myself busy and think about what comes next, like a rainbow after a long, hard rain. I'm spending my time focusing on what makes me special. Like the smell of the earth and the air after it's rained. Fresh. Full of possibility and hope.

Hannah Cecil was born in 2005 and went to school in Oklahoma. Now she's an author, looking forward to the future she will create. She's finishing high school, after which she will receive her driver's license. She has a job and is saving money so she can afford her own place. Hannah loves the earth and is at ease with the trees, plants, flowers, and bees. The rest of her biography is being lived and yet to come. She'd love for you to check in on her!

www.instagram.com/h4nn4h_belle/

Barbara Von Schmeling

The Warrior Goddess

When I was first invited to write this chapter, I felt honored. I also had the thought that I have not been to *real darkness* in my life. Nevertheless, I believe I have taken the lightness that I graciously received from the creator and shared it with those around me. I sometimes playfully say: I must have gone through a lot in my past lives, because this is a pretty good one! That acknowledgment is based on my belief that we are spiritual beings capable of having multiple human experiences. So what does it mean to have "a pretty good one" this time around? For me, it begins with the body I chose to inhabit, the experiences I've been through, and the family I chose to belong to. When I say I chose (again, my belief) I mean that coming into this planet and living this particular life is a conscious choice to evolve as a soul. Nothing is given to us as a punishment or reward, but rather what we choose to go through to grow, evolve, or simply contribute. Coming back to my life, I was born and raised in Brazil, to a beautiful family of parents and grandparents who had been in love for as long as I can remember until the day they left this planet. They were my role models for what an intimate relationship is all about. They helped me envision a passionate relationship, and I always had the conviction that I would be able to create that for myself. Perhaps having that conviction allowed me to manifest the man I have in my life today and the relationship we've built. My Sergio, my love, my soulmate, the man I love, admire, worship, and adore! He is the one who lights my heart and soul on fire with his presence. He is the one who created the safe space for me to be myself, to love with no limits, to surrender. His beautiful masculine self allows me to trust, to receive, and to simply be…and that I had to learn to do, or better yet, I had to remember to "be." For years I tried so hard to connect to my masculine energy. I thought being feminine was a sign of weakness, but that was because I had the wrong idea of what femininity truly was. Allow me to elaborate on that. Every human being is born with masculine and feminine energy, and we all have a dominant core energy. For women, usually that energy is the feminine, and for men it is the masculine. Although I grew up seeing how my parents and grandparents interacted, I allowed myself to buy into the idea that we, as women, must be completely independent and achieve as much as we can to feel successful. That is a model of success based on masculine energy traits, as the masculine is the energy that makes us move toward an outcome, get organized, focus, get things done, persevere, and achieve what we set our minds to. It brings out our inner warrior.

Don't get me wrong, these are incredible skills to develop, and I believe they are necessary for every human being. Actually, martial arts helped me connect to that beautiful side of me, and those traits have been imprinted in me since my journey started, back in 1993. The challenge for most women is tapping too much into that energy and forgetting our true nature. When that happens, although we feel accomplished, we also feel depleted, exhausted, and, somehow, not whole. The deep connection to the feminine is something I had to learn and cultivate after years of pushing myself to be more connected to my masculine side. I mean, I'm a martial arts Master, instructor, and competitor; of course I need to be tough! I'm a business owner; of course I need to make things happen! I'm a leader in my company; of course I need to be strong! But my feminine self was calling for help. She would show up in unexpected moments, as in the middle of teaching a class, when a child would get kicked. I knew I was supposed to push them to keep going, but deep inside I wanted to hug them and wipe off their tears. Or when I would choose to sit down and talk to another woman with no agenda other than to simply connect. Or during a little girl's first lesson, after the father shared how challenging she could be, then at the end he hugged her and said how proud he was. My heart would burst open and I'd feel so deeply I couldn't contain my tears. That is the feminine—the energy of love, empathy, connection, intuition, caring, and grace. Why was I suppressing her? Why did I think she was weak when she was actually my superpower? Probably because I didn't know what she really was, and by suppressing her I was losing the unique gifts and qualities that set me apart. I knew I needed to surrender to her beauty and power.

In 2014 I brought a child into this world. My Annabella, my biggest gift, the light and joy of my life! I feel I need a whole chapter just for her. I thought I had so much to teach her, but once she came, I realized I was the one who had so much to learn. She is my wisest teacher. Three days before she was born, I left work and said, "I will see you in two weeks." I had no idea what I was saying. When I first felt her presence outside of my body, I became a whole new person. Actually, when I first found out she was in my womb, I became a different person. In that instant, my world completely shifted! My heart opened like never before, and the level of love I experienced was like nothing I ever anticipated. I know every mother says the same, and they are right. As the structured and disciplined person I was, it was very clear in my mind how I wanted to raise her, what values I wanted to instill in her, and the person I would like her to grow up to be. Of course, I knew martial arts was going to be part of her life, and it was nonnegotiable! I wanted her to develop that warrior spirit, to be able to stand up for herself and achieve anything she wants in life. I knew the discipline I acquired was something I wanted her to develop, and I still believe it's an extremely important skill to practice. But I also recognized she had a beautiful princess inside of her, and I just couldn't ignore her essence. She wears her heart on her sleeve, and her spirit is so free, and by embracing that in her, I also found this essence in myself! My awakening occurred because I felt there was a part of me missing. I trained to be a warrior, just like many women around me, not only in martial arts but as business owners, mothers, or women who are the main provider for their families. What we all share in common is a lack of deep connection to our feminine essence. Being a warrior, hustling, pushing ourselves, we end up forgetting our nature as a woman, which is to nurture, to connect, to live the moment, and to simply be. I went through a stage where my mind was fighting my heart. I thought I had to go back to work, to prove my worth as a woman; after all, being a warrior was my identity, but deep inside I was so conflicted! What I really wanted was to raise my child, love my husband, and enjoy the beautiful family we created. I felt I would be judged if I chose that path, and the first person judging me was myself. So I would push through and go to work, only to feel I was leaving a piece of my heart and soul behind, and that would lead to guilt and emptiness. Until I decided to accept and embrace the Goddess within me, after which I felt so free and whole.

Annabella has been a gift in so many ways, one of which was to wake me up to my true self so I could feel whole as a woman and get me started on the path of helping other women find the same in themselves. Following that awakening, there was a series of events that led me to get curious and take a dive deep into this new way of living. That is when Feminine Freedom was born. It is my passion and mission to guide women to that awakening, to realize there is more to life than what they have been experiencing, and to open them up to the possibility of feeling fully alive—body, heart, mind, and soul connected. To be clear, it has nothing to do with motherhood; it has everything to do with embracing and expanding the full capacity of our being. It's about remembering who we are by removing the layers of conditioning we've been through, the limiting beliefs we create, and the expectations of others or ourselves, and by allowing our nature to be fully expressed in all its beauty and grace. That is available to all of us. My invitation would be for you to start by simply slowing down in your life and becoming more present in your body. That helps connect you to your senses, as sensuality is an important part of the feminine. Embracing your emotions and finding healthy outlets for them, as holding them in doesn't serve you. Practicing to receive! I know we are programmed to do everything for others, but the only way you will be able to give is if you have it in yourself first.

I live now with a very clear understanding of who I am, and I'm totally in love with that woman! I learned the power that lies in my essence and the bliss that I feel by being in that place. I embrace all parts of me and access each of them when I need to. I learned not only to do but also to be. I am conscious that the masculine in me makes life happen, but the feminine makes my life worth living. I'm not letting go of "her" ever again. If you haven't found the Goddess in your Warrior, I hope you do. You and your life will be forever transformed.

Barbara Von Schmeling • The Warrior Goddess

Barbara Von Schmeling is a wife, mother, business owner, and advocate for women's wellness, personal growth, and feminine expression. She's the founder of Feminine Freedom, which offers a combination of feminine embodiment, healing, and relationship guidance. Her mission is to awaken women to the power of their Divine Feminine essence, guiding them to a journey of self-love and awareness, and helping them move past their challenges and release energy that might be holding them back. By finding the freedom in expressing who they really are, women develop a better relationship with their bodies, their partners, and everyone around them. Barbara is a 7th degree Black Belt Master, multiple time World Champion, and co-owner of Victory Martial Arts. What makes her unique is teaching harmony between the Divine Masculine and Feminine. She believes the ability to shift seamlessly from one to the other is the key to living a harmonious life, where every woman can feel whole and fulfilled.

www.thefemininefreedom.com
www.facebook.com/TheFeminineFreedom
www.facebook.com/groups/thefemininefreedom/
www.instagram.com/thefemininefreedom/

Jenn Lockhart

The Gift of Desperation

About seven years ago I was working as a waitress at a cute little diner in Longmont, Colorado. It was seven in the morning, we had just opened, and I was hungover. I had a smile on my face like I always did, but if you were present enough and looked deep into my eyes, you could see that I was hurting inside. I was a new mom, I was married, I was overweight, and I was depressed. I would numb the pain I felt inside every night with alcohol. I would wake up, go to work, come home, drink, and do it all over again, every day. This was the vicious cycle I was stuck in for many years.

There was this man who would eat breakfast at the diner almost every morning. He had a lot of friends, a lot of money, a lot of time, and a beautiful family. He was sober, and he appeared to always be really, really happy. I didn't know what he did for work, but I knew he was successful and that he had the life I wanted, so I always kept my eyes on him. I knew he always kept his eyes on me too.

He could see right through me. He could see the pain behind my eyes and through the fake smile on my face. He knew I needed help. He never came right out and said it, but he would always say things to me like, "Jenn, when you're ready to change your life, come talk to me." And that was it. I turned down his offer more times than I can count, even though I was hurting and desperate for help.

On that particular morning, though, something was different. Can you think of a time in your life when you made a decision that changed the course of your life forever? Something happened that caused you to get there, whether it was something that physically happened or a feeling that you had. Some people call this rock bottom, when you get so desperate for change that you will do *anything* to make it happen. I was at that point. I didn't know what I needed, but what I was doing wasn't working for me anymore. I had hit my rock bottom.

That morning when he made his offer, I said, "*Yes*. Let's talk." For the first time, I was ready to drop my ego, take some action, and finally admit, not just to him but also to myself, that I needed help. After work that day, I went to his office, and he sat me down on a chair in an almost empty room with white boards hung on the walls. There was a bookshelf in the corner and more chairs stacked up in the back of the room. On those boards he wrote out a bunch of stuff, but really all I could see were four big letters staring me in the face. HOPE. That afternoon, he shared with me his own personal rags-to-riches story. That was when I began to believe that change was possible for me too.

Without hesitation, I decided it was time to jump into the unknown and do something different. I was scared, but I was desperate for change. That afternoon, I signed up to become part of this man's company, and he became my mentor. I signed up for his trainings and showed up at his weekly meetings. I plugged in. I was excited.

My life did not change instantly, but I had faith that if I just stuck with the process and kept showing up, I would eventually see it happen. Or I could quit and go back to living the life I was so desperate to escape; that was *not* an option.

I found myself surrounded by inspiring people who were seeking more out of their lives. Some were farther along than I was. I decided to start modeling their behaviors: reading, watching personal growth videos on YouTube, being more positive on social media, upgrading my self-care, and starting a daily gratitude journal. I even got my son involved in doing gratitude with me. He was three at the time, and most days his gratitude was for dinosaurs, PAW Patrol, mommy, daddy, and our dog, Annie. It was the cutest thing.

Looking back, I can see that I'd spent most my time focused on all the negatives in my life, which is why I was so depressed. I was blind to all the beauty. The daily gratitude was a great way for me to start training my brain to focus on and actually see the good that surrounded me. The truth is, there will always be good and there will always be bad, but what you decide to focus on really does determine how you feel, which dictates the actions you do or do not take. Gratitude is really *that* important.

I pushed myself to do more things outside my comfort zone, like live Facebook videos. I showed up at different events, alone, feeling better about myself every time for doing things that in my head seemed so scary but in reality weren't so bad. They were actually kind of fun. I kept repeating to myself, "Jenn, nothing changes if nothing changes. If you want different, you must do different."

I celebrated every victory, big or small, even if it was just me celebrating alone in my head. Every setback I had—and *yes*, I had a bunch—brought new growth. Those setbacks motivated me. I learned that I must set goals, then learned the *big* message: it's not necessarily about achieving every goal; it is about enjoying the journey and loving who you are becoming in the process.

My confidence began to grow, and my attitude toward life was new. I learned to love myself again—or maybe for the first time. I pulled myself out of the dark place that came with being overweight, depressed, angry, and frustrated, mainly with myself, but I blamed others as well. There were good moments, but in my dark time I focused on all the shit in my life. I let my negative self-talk dictate my actions, like spending days in bed feeling sorry for myself. I wasn't present. I wasn't grateful. I'd chug vodka out of a bottle hidden in an old purse in my closet to numb myself from all the pain and to avoid the perceived expectations I had put on myself. No one could live up to those expectations. I felt alone when I was feeling depressed and drinking all the time, but when I eventually got sober, I felt even more alone. Which came three years after I said yes to the man at the diner.

My sobriety meant I lost some of my close friends, and eventually my husband. I was outgrowing my old life. The changes I was going through made me reevaluate the standards I had for myself and for those around me.

Another mentor of mine told me, "Jenn, circle change is necessary for growth. You will find new people who are more aligned with who you are and where you are headed." I blindly kept faith that she was right, and, slowly but surely, I began to find my new tribe.

All I ever really wanted was to be loved, accepted, and validated by others. What I found instead was that true happiness only comes when you learn to *fully love, accept, and validate yourself*. It's kind of simple.

- Do things that contribute to your happiness and fulfillment.
- Push yourself in order to grow.
- Stop trying to please or live up to every perceived, unrealistic expectation.
- Consciously surround yourself with people who are more aligned with your newfound authenticity.
- Take off the masks you've been hiding behind for so many years. Show your real smile!
- Choose to learn to love yourself and live your own authentic life. Discover the freedom of just being yourself, whether

people like it or not.

Today, I've never felt better. I am a divorced, single mom, sober, healthier than ever, and in love with my life. I'm focused on continuing to grow myself and on bringing more love, understanding, and deeper truth to those around me.

That morning at the diner changed my life, not because of what the man offered me, but because it was the first time I decided to choose courage over comfort, and faith over fear. It was the first time I said yes to stepping outside the box I put myself in. It was the first time I said yes to me. The ripple effect has been priceless.

Regardless of where you are right now, just know that at any point you can choose to make a change. I felt stuck for a very long time, but I am proof that you can overcome limiting beliefs. You can overcome your fear of judgment, and you can eighty-six the feeling of not being good enough. You can choose to stop listening to others. You can choose to stop trying to please everyone around you. You can choose to follow your dreams. You can choose to start creating a life you actually love living. It's your choice. All it takes is a decision.

Jenn Lockhart • The Gift of Desperation

Jenn Lockhart completely transformed her life. She went from being an overweight, depressed alcoholic with a poor mindset to loving her life to the fullest every day and coaching others on how to do the same. For almost a decade, Jenn has attended personal growth seminars, read books, gotten into nature, eaten healthier foods, and become mindful of who and what gets her attention. She consciously surrounds herself with people who inspire her, and she learns how to love herself by meditating, attending masterminds, journaling, keeping her emotions in check, and facing challenges head-on with the intent to grow. Currently living in Colorado with her son, Cameron, she wants nothing more than for him to feel consistent joy and happiness and to love the life he is living. Jenn believes that life it too short to sit still and too damn long to settle for anything less than what your heart truly desires.

linkr.bio/JennLockhart?fbclid=IwAR3JU7DcZNlvW9Ge2nTn6ljv0vZ-VWJx0irJ8O5ZwUHYKEHzAj9lvo_T9KmI

Jessica Garza

Actions Speak Louder than Words

Motherhood. What can I say, it has been my greatest teacher. I wasn't exactly a planner when it came to having my kids. I have two girls, both teenagers at the time that I am writing this. I married when I was eighteen, and three years later welcomed our first sweet girl. Six years later we started over with her little sister. Neither were "planned," and they both came exactly at the perfect time—when we least expected it and weren't ready. I have often said that I have literally grown up with my kids because I was such a kid when I first became a mother, and, quite frankly, I wouldn't have it any other way.

Growing up with my kids has been fun and hard. It has been both rewarding and dreadful. There have been days when I have felt like I can't seem to get anything right. Sometimes I look up at the sky and smirk at my Creator like, "Seriously, you couldn't have sent me an instructions manual with this one?" Other days I wonder if I have completely screwed them up; and yet on occasion I sometimes feel like Super Mom. I get to experience the full range of emotions, and my life is filled with variety because I am their mom. Hands down, my job as a mom has taught me more about myself than any other relationship I am a part of.

When I first became a mom, I thought that it was my job to create the perfect human, so I got right to work. Correcting her every "mistake," rewarding her for a job well done when she did things the way *I liked them to be done.* You know, programming her little brain to be just like me. Except she isn't me! Which brings me to my first aha moment as a mom. My daughter did not come here to be like me; she came here to be her. It is not my job to create a perfect anything, as perfection does not exist.

When I realized that I am not here to make my daughters be like me, or anyone else for that matter, it stopped me in my tracks. Wait, how much of what I was training her to be was what I would even want for myself? This sent me on a road to self-discovery: aka, growing up with my kids. I was figuring out who I was while teaching them to do the same. Here's the deal, kids don't listen to what you say. *Kids learn what they live.*

I remember a time when my daughter was having issues with people at school. She didn't feel like she fit in with any of the "groups" at her new middle school. Before I knew it, she had completely changed. The clothes she wore, the conversations she was having, the way she treated people; it was alarming. I quickly realized that she was sacrificing the most authentic version of herself in order to "fit in." What made matters worse was when I asked the question "Why would she do that?" the answer was not an easy one. It was because she had seen me do the same thing time and time again. She knew the real me at home, but she saw me change my persona depending on who I was around in order to have "friends," and now she was doing the same thing. My children have been such amazing mirrors to show me exactly how I am living. They reflect it right back to me in the way that they live their lives. In their friendships, their hardships, their beliefs, their dreams, their fears, it is such a gift (when I choose to see it that way).

After the middle school experience, I vowed to consciously parent my girls. To have my eyes and heart wide open, willing to be wrong, with humility and grace for me and for them. I quickly realized that my girls have their own internal compass. They have their own beliefs about what is right and wrong. My job is to be an example of how they can access and use that internal compass for their own True North; this was not an easy task because of what I had previously modeled for them during their youngest, most impressionable years.

When I was upset about something, I would bury those feelings deep down and use it a fuel for whatever came next. If I needed ammunition for my next argument with their dad, I used it for that. If I needed to excel at work, I used it to push myself to the next level. I powered through and plowed through my emotions because I saw crying as a sign of weakness. When they were little, if they fell down, I told them to get up and brush it off. "Put your big-girl panties on" was my favorite thing to tell them. There was no room for weakness (emotions) in our family.

Looking back, I realize that through my actions and expectations of them, I created little soldiers. They were just doing exactly what I was modeling for them. With this new awareness, I began to see how hard this was for them. No matter what they were feeling, they would shove it down and just keep going. I took a new look at the way I was parenting them and realized that if they were just modeling what they had seen me (and their dad) do, they wouldn't know how to feel.

My oldest daughter pushed herself to excel in the school setting. Her life was filled with praise for her grades from a very young age. When she brought home a report card filled with As, we celebrated as a family. She chose to attend a high school that required their students to graduate with both a high school diploma and an Associate in Fine Arts degree from a local community college. She barely saw the sun for four years while she plowed through the rigorous work required to pull that off. Am I proud? Yes, of course. But it wasn't until her sophomore year that I realized what had been created through our actions over the years. Through rewarding her for her grades all her life, she equated so much of her self-worth to what her teacher's grade book said. If her GPA dropped below a 4.0, she got stressed out and would stay up later and later to study more and more. I realized we had trained her to believe that she had to prove something in order to be worthy of our love. We had created a measuring system for how worthy she felt. Of course this isn't what we intended, but it is definitely what was created.

All of this made me take a real look at myself. What was I using to measure my worth? My work? The number of things I could get done in one day? My value was tied to things that no one cared about except me. It was all just a figment of my imagination to think that if I did more stuff, or filled our calendar with more things to do, then I would be worthy of my family's love. If my kids looked perfect, with their perfect grades, then I would be impressive in some way. I cringe just thinking about that now.

Retraining myself to love myself for no other reason than because I am me is what has made all the difference for my kids as well. Through experiencing me in this way, they now model this healthier behavior. Loving themselves unconditionally, there is no longer a measuring system in our household. The only standard is, "Are you in alignment with yourself, and are you doing your best?"

They now see me in my truest form, which gives them permission to do the same. When I am at my best and when I am at my worst and everything in between. They experience me in all of it. I do not hide anything from them. When I am sad, they see me sad. When I am mad, I am mad. (But don't spew that anger *at* people... that's what punching bags are for.) When I do something that doesn't feel right, I apologize. I offer help. I say no! I experience it all, and they get to see that. No matter what I model for them, there are lessons in it for them. Rather than attempting to control the narrative by *telling* them how to feel, I aim to help them process what *they* are actually feeling in healthy ways. I model what it's like to be an emotional human who feels all she feels.

Motherhood has taught me so much! It has taught me how to feel, how to love, how to love myself, and how to receive love from others. Above all, it has taught me that my actions speak louder than my words.

Jessica Garza • Actions Speak Louder than Words

Jessica Garza is a forever-evolving human who lives in Texas with her husband and kids. She has an insatiable hunger for truth and a passion for relationships. She was married twice and divorced once, all to the same man. As a result of these unique experiences, Jess decided to study relationships by interviewing successful partnerships, reading books, attending seminars, and putting what she's learned into practice in her own relationships. Now, having spent the last decade learning through publications and practice what it takes to create a successful relationship, she shares her knowledge and passion for relationships with those who may be struggling in the ways she struggled in the past. Her hope is to save others the heartache of learning the hard way. She believes that relationships are the single most important part of the human experience and aims to share all she has learned in the most streamlined way possible.

http://www.nurelationships.com
https://www.facebook.com/JessGarza13

Trina Ward

The Heart Don't Change

Country life was the only life I knew growing up, and the same holds true today. I've watched my parents and grandparents slaughter the hogs and beef, cure and store the meat, tend laying hens, cultivate gardens and orchards, and maintain water wells for drinking water.

I was tagged a back-road country girl and that was fine with me. I would go to the hay field with my grandpa and ride the old green tractor fender, letting my cowboy boots hit the knobs on the tires while holding on for dear life and being his eyes if anything went wrong. He always took along a fishing pole so I could catch a grasshopper and fish before and after working. On the way home I would hear the stories of his childhood and early adulthood working in the potato and peanut fields. I hold those stories dear to my heart today.

My family owned a tract of land where my grandparents raised their kids, then my dad and his brother also made their family homes there, so growing up with family was definitely a blessing for all of us. I am delighted to say I still own the property.

I have memories of the storm clouds rolling in, and we would all go to my grandparents' and pile in the handmade rock cellar with a huge wooden door. This is where my grandma had all her canned goods along with beds for us kids to sleep on. My grandma is the one who taught me to quilt and to can vegetables. She was gruff but a kind and caring soul. We had a special bond that I cherish.

My family would plan a monthly trip to the nearest town to get the necessities and then drive back home on the long dirt road with the windows rolled down, letting the balmy air blow to cool us down. I could walk up and down the dirt roads, ride our bikes to a place called Fox Hill where we would ride down the hill and push the bikes back up, just to do it all over again for hours (barefoot). This was our entertainment along with fishing in the ponds and going to school and playing ball. We had family gatherings on Sundays with a big dinner and my dad playing the guitar and my cousins and I playing Wiffle ball in the yard. My parents had a truly happy, loyal, supportive marriage. Mom was fifteen when they married, and they would have had their sixty-fifth anniversary this year, were they still with us. Their love was true, they were pillars of our community, and they were the parents to all our friends in school. To this day, I have never heard anything detrimental about them. They were my biggest supporters my whole life and continue to play a big part in my day-to-day thoughts and decisions.

I have many wonderful memories, like lying in the back of the old farm truck on one of my grandma's handmade quilts watching for falling stars, looking for the Big Dipper, the Little Dipper, and the Milky Way. Or snagging a fruit jar and poking holes in the lid to catch fireflies. My greatest people were family—my mom and dad, my sister and brother, my grandparents and my aunts, uncles, and cousins. We were all we had and were the only ones we were around. Our cousins were our best friends, and our aunts and uncles were our second parents. We were all part of the same big heart, *a heart that don't change, tho the times do.*

My dad set up a basketball goal in our dirt yard and worked with me for hours, which resulted in me being a part of my high school team that was #1 in Class B in Oklahoma. My dad also set up a one-gallon can and had me practice throwing my fishing lure in the can from thirty feet away so I could make great casts where I needed to catch a fish. My mom made homemade donuts and breads and jams and cooked the most amazing country meals. We always had a clean and comfortable home, and she and my dad were always there for us.

As we all grew older, our mindsets changed, and our destiny remained unknown. We still dream and plan, but the force of change is inevitable. We make decisions we think are best for us, and then the big thing called *life* throws us into a whirlwind that lasts until we make the next decision to get out of the tornado and live life again. It is not easy working a full-time job, taking kids to seventy-five baseball games a summer, then school and school ball, keeping a house presentable, preparing meals, finishing the laundry, and taking care of our own cattle and farm animals. We send our hogs and beef to the slaughterhouse and try to find time to go pick up the end products in thirty days. There's no time for a garden, so Sunday dinners are driving through a fast-food place while on your way to your next destination. The important thing is that we spend time with our greatest people. This is what makes us happy—our kids, our livelihood, our life. Country life fills us up. It is who we are.

Like many other folks, we've had losses. I lost my sister at an early age, then my grandparents, my mom and dad, the best mother-in-law, and many other loved ones in a very short period of time. We lost a grandbaby, and we have a grandbaby who was only given a 3 percent chance to live; that grandbaby is now seven months old.

Grief is part of life. For many years I let grief keep me from enjoying my blessings; then my eyes opened and I realized that my blessings should not become dormant because of my grief. Blessings, sunshine, rainy days, green pastures, birds singing, cattle grazing, great family and great friends are all blessings that God has given us to be grateful for and enjoy.

I have the most amazing soulmate/husband that anyone could ever dream of. We are truly *one*. He has been my rock through everything imaginable. We can think for one another and complete each other's sentences. We work together every minute, whether we are on the ranch or at the office. He is an amazing musician. A perfectionist. The sunshine to my storm and the joy to my heart. He is the hardest working man I have ever seen, and he never stops dreaming. He is a provider, not only for us but for anyone in need. He loves me unconditionally and is truly my heart and soul.

We have five children and nineteen grandchildren. We are proud of our children and the lives they have. They are all good-hearted and kind people. Our grandchildren are truly our life, and we are now chasing them to summer ballgames and loving every minute of it. We just hope we continue to be their greatest people. We have a big firepit overlooking our ranch, and we enjoy a quiet evening with a fire while we look for the Little Dipper and the Big Dipper and the Milky Way, always watching for fireflies and reminiscing. We are grateful to be part of the memories of our kids and grandkids, grateful they know the magic of the firefly and where to find the Milky Way and Big and Little Dippers.

Life is truly just a vapor, from infancy through childhood, from teenager to adulthood, then parenthood to grandparenthood—it all slips by like a flash. Enjoyment is ours if we choose it. The soul melts a little, life goes on, but *the heart don't change*. I have chosen to enjoy my life, my country life, my husband, family and friends, and all the moments that are never lost or forgotten. Sometimes the days are dark and dreary, but there's always the moon and the stars and a sun. Even when we don't see them, they are there giving us the hope to continue on and shine our light.

I believe that if we always follow our heart, it will never steer us wrong. Sometimes we get off the path, but *once a good heart, always a good heart*. Our minds change, our bodies change, we get bitter and cold, sometimes it even seems like our hearts have changed, but from childhood, we develop our mindset and the feelings that we live with for the rest of our lives. We are country with big hearts, and I will always be a back-road country girl. The soul melts a little, but life goes on, and *the heart don't change.*

Trina Ward • The Heart Don't Change

Trina Ward and her husband Ricky own and operate RE/MAX offices in two different counties in Eastern Oklahoma. They find joy helping others fulfill their dreams with a new recreational property or a ranch or a home in town. They are among the top brokers/agents in Oklahoma with RE/MAX Champion Land Brokers. They also own and operate W2 Ranch where they raise Black Angus and Wagyu cattle, bale hay, feed cows, build fences, brush hog, and do all the maintenance. They live life to the fullest, taking pride and finding joy in helping their kids, grandkids, family, and friends.

www.facebook.com/RemaxChampionLandBrokers
tward@remax.net
www.clbrealestate.com

Mary Lee Handley

How to Grow a Legacy

The kiss of the sun for pardon,
The song of the birds for mirth,
One is nearer God's heart in a garden
Than anywhere else on earth.
- Dorothy Frances Gurney

My first gardening experiences came from my mother and maternal grandmother. They instilled in me the love of all flowers, vegetables, trees, and nature in general. They took immense pride in their homes and yards. My grandmother's primary garden consisted only of rosebushes. She and my grandfather tended them with love and care. They had every color, and many were heirlooms. They also had violets, hens and chicks, pansies, tulips, daffodils, johnny jump ups, and more, all in flower beds around the house.

My mother had a different kind of garden in our backyard. It consisted of many fruit trees: banana, Ponderosa lemon, grapefruit, and orange! Along the fence line she had rose of Sharon, and next to our home she had peach trees and fig trees. The street was lined with bougainvillea. We had beautiful trees that lined the driveway, and two in the front yard—I wish I could remember what kind. All along the front of the house she had elephant ears. It remains the most beautiful yard I've ever seen.

I inherited their green thumbs and put them to use years later when I had my own home. I, too, wanted a beautiful yard. I planted a tree and lots of flowers. Soon, I had my own vegetable garden. I started out small with the veggies and worked it into a bigger garden, adding varieties each season.

I had several varieties of roses and spring flowers (daffodils, lily of the valley, and tulips). When I moved several years later, I took my Tropicana rosebush with me and replanted her. She still survives today and is about forty years old. Her flowers have faded, but her blooms remain fragrant.

I still garden today! I have flowers and add more every year. My vegetable garden gets better year after year. Before I plant, I like to know which plants are compatible and which ones like flowers and herbs planted beside them. I like to water in the morning and always at the base of the plants. I talk to my plants and even name some of them. Some of the plants' blooms like to be tickled. You do this by gently flicking the blooms. It also helps with the plant fertilization process. It's important to pluck the suckers at the base of the plants to help keep them healthy. The healthier the plant, the higher the yield.

The best part of this story is that my son and I worked the gardens together for years. We learned from each other. This was our peaceful place, our joyful place. He taught me to research and know my plants. He taught me to rotate the plants so they would get the nutrients they need to survive. He taught me to talk to them nicely every day. He taught me how to make pickles from my cucumbers and how to keep the veggies fresh. He taught me to only use organic *everything*!

It wasn't all work and no play in the garden. We talked about everything. He loved his family, his work, his friends. He loved gardening, cooking, and fishing. And he loved God, too. We were in our happy place, in our element. We shared the same love and respect for nature, humankind, and love for all God's creations.

Bryan's niche was cooking. He planned his meals and meticulously chose the foods he would prepare. He made everything from scratch! Most of the foods he prepared were grown in our garden. He especially enjoyed preparing Asian and Thai foods.

The herbs we grew were peppermint, Thai basil, sweet basil, rosemary, dill, oregano, and chives. We dried and bottled our herbs for future use. The aromas were heavenly.

He learned much of his cooking information by watching cooking shows, and by trial and error. He had his own style. He enjoyed cooking salmon, fresh tuna steaks, briskets, a variety of sauces, fresh homemade pies, and smoothies. I wish I had his recipes, but they were saved in his memory. He didn't have time to share.

My son passed away unexpectedly last year. My garden keeps his memory alive. It keeps me alive. Bryan and I loved being in the kitchen too! With all the tomatoes, peppers, okra, and cucumbers we had harvested from our garden, we had to decide what we would do first. We pickled everything but the tomatoes. We had an abundance of okra, so some were pickled, some were frozen, and some were cooked. We made salsa for taco night, and stewed tomatoes with garlic and onions for stew on chilly winter nights. The cucumbers were made into bread-and-butter pickles, dill pickles, and spicy pickles. We pickled peppers. Sometimes we tied ribbons on jars and tucked them neatly under the Christmas tree as gifts.

We also baked bread: banana nut bread and zucchini pineapple bread with walnuts (his favorites), which were also given as gifts. We would sing and joke, and sometimes he would take my hand and decide it was time for a little dance. He was such a jovial fellow.

Sometimes I sit outside with the plants and nature and simply admire the beauty. It inspires me to do more. It inspires me to love life more, to respect it, and to love nature and all it enfolds.

Every November you will find me planning the next spring's planting. I can't wait to get down and dirty. Just getting my hands in the dirt, feeling Mother Earth in my hands. This excites me. And spring, oh beautiful spring. The birds singing, trees budding, sprigs of grass and flowers showing their little heads above the soil's surface, bringing new life to a new season.

This year, by request, I've started vegetable seeds for two of my daughters for their community garden. I recently had about two hundred and fifty starters in my living room.

One of my grandsons is now a horticulturist who says I inspired him to love and respect plants. He now has a very lucrative business because of how he loves and respects the plants.

One of my granddaughters is planning her gardens—flowers, plants, and vegetables. This gives me joy.

When I need alone time, I know where to go. My garden gives me peace, joy, and love. It gives me memories of days gone by, the people who have inspired my love for plants, and my desire to grow in all ways—in my life, my relationships, my hopes and dreams. Just like my plants grow, I will grow too. And be nourished, just as my plants nourish. I have lavender and sage for the bees, butterflies, and hummingbirds. I have hanging plants and plants in pots. I have plants all through the house. I even have "foster" plants for one of my children! It's no wonder spring is my favorite time, my favorite season. It's a healing time. A peaceful time. A time to enjoy all things new and wonderful!

I search and seek for what Mother Earth and nature have given me. Come with me into my garden and look into the windows of my mind. The beauty of the plants. The buzzing of the bees as they gather nectar from the blooms, and the fluttering of the butterflies in the wind to visit the fragrant flowers. Oh, the sweet aroma is intoxicating! As I sit, I watch the birds gathering the string and twigs and straw that I've left for them to build their nests. I enjoy listening to them chatter to each other on a fine spring day. And the gentle rain falling to clean the earth. The fragrance after the rain is so comforting.

Writing my story helped me realize that I want to leave my family a legacy. Something to remember me by. A legacy is about passion. For me, it's gardening, and it could be for you. Discover what it's like to grow your own food, to learn about what you grow and how all things work and come together. *Discover how to grow a legacy* that can be shared for generations to come, just as it was by the generations before. I share my passion for growth and new beginnings with each of you, to help you learn to *grow your own legacy.*

Mary Lee Handley Reed was born August 22nd, 1948, in Harlingen, Texas. She attended schools in Raymondville and Lubbock, Texas, graduating from Lubbock Christian High School. She studied Physical Therapy in Texas and Oklahoma. She also worked in insurance and for Akins Natural Foods in Oklahoma. She lives in Yukon, Oklahoma, with her husband, Ron Reed. She has one daughter, Heidi; a son, Bryan, who passed in 2021; a foster daughter who passed in her teens; three stepchildren (one deceased); twelve grandchildren; and six great-grandchildren with a seventh on the way. Mary Lee graciously takes over as mother to others who need it. She is a cancer survivor and spends her free time reading, gardening, and winter baking. She loves the company of her children, grandchildren, and great-grandchildren. And Misti.

www.facebook.com/mary.l.handley/

Roxy Feller

My Dearest Jessica

I remember the first time I heard the words, "you are a product of your environment." It freaked me out! You were less than a year old, and if that statement were true, then I had some serious work to do on myself. There was no way in hell I wanted you growing up the way that I grew up. I also knew that "I" was "your" environment. I wanted your upbringing to be different than mine. I felt the environment I was raised in was dysfunctional. I knew it hadn't always been a fun way to live.

I felt the humiliation of standing in the "free lunch" line or using food stamps while at our small-town grocery store. I prayed a school friend wouldn't walk in and see me at the checkout line. I was humiliated living off welfare, having to moving all of the time, always being the new kid trying to fit in. I was an expert at survival techniques and knew there was no way I was going to pass them on to you. I knew I had to get my shit together or you would grow up feeling limited, as I had. I wanted you to grow up excited about your opportunities.

The best way to describe me at that time with my ingrained survival techniques is what I refer to as "the polished apple syndrome," where everything on the outside is shiny like a perfect apple but the inside is rotten to the core. For me, rotten meant being insecure, self-sabotaging, people-pleasing, verbally abusive to self, addicted to being unhappy, a victim, lacking belief in myself—you name it and I was living it. "I" was a product of "my" environment.

Everything did look pretty on the outside. I married your dad, the most popular boy in school. We were a great-looking couple, we lived in a nice home, we drove nice vehicles. It was a picture-perfect life. Except the outside did not match what was going on in the inside. I thought it was his job to make me happy, and, damn it, he wasn't doing a very good job of it! I didn't realize how addicted I was to negativity and unhappiness. I was comfortable there. They were familiar to me. This is what worried—and motivated—me the most. My negative mindset. I didn't want you growing up thinking it is normal to give your power away, or that other people are in charge of making you happy, or that it is their fault if you are unhappy with your life.

Jessica, my sweet angel, I knew I was a mess on the inside. Until you came into my life, I didn't have the courage to make the changes I needed for myself. I knew that I had to change for myself, and I had to protect you from our lineage of dysfunction. I had to protect you from the self-sabotaging behaviors. I had to protect you from being like me.

I began to work hard on myself. Sometimes I knew what I was doing, and sometimes I didn't. I devoured books. I attended seminars. I hired my first coach. His name was Bob Proctor. He was in the movie and the book called *The Secret*. He said, "Roxy, you need to get out of your own way." What did that even mean? I would say, "Tell me what to do and I will do it." He didn't tell me. He guided me. He was exactly what I needed to help me to begin to transform my life.

I loved what I was learning from Bob, so I decided to get my coaching certification through him and his company. For the first fifteen years, I didn't do much with it. I still lacked belief in myself, and after your dad and I got divorced, I was a single mommy who was not only taking care of you but now your little sister, Josie.

It was more important than ever for me to learn, grow, stretch, and move outside my limitations. I learned about the Law of Attraction and other universal laws. I learned that what you think about, you bring about, and that your thoughts create your belief system, which ultimately drives outcomes and results. The most important thing I learned: *If you don't like your life, you must change your thinking, which will change your belief system.*

I started to think differently. I started doing affirmations to retrain my unconscious mind. I started doing affirmations with both of you girls. I knew if I taught you both at an early age what I was learning in my thirties that it would be the beginning of breaking the pattern and change our family tree.

Outcomes in my life started changing because I started changing. Instead of a victim mentality, I had a victor mentality. I was taking my mess and turning it into a message. I started coaching men and women to get the results that I was getting. I was teaching people how to have a mindset that helped them have better lives and not be victims to their circumstances.

You and Josie were learning as I learned. We found new language, telling ourselves to "get connected," which meant being in the vibration of love, joy, happiness, and abundance as much as humanly possible. When an argument would happen between you girls or from a not-so-fun day at school, I would remind you to *get connected*. I taught you girls that you are in charge or your happiness, that you can either focus on the things you don't want in life that show up *or* you can create your life by design and have the life you truly want.

With all of the work I have done on myself, I am seeing that the "Polished Apple Syndrome" will no longer be a part of my DNA, and that I have broken the thread for generations to come, that my daughters are now a product of *that* environment.

When my father passed away and I could barely get off the couch, Josie wrote me a letter reminding me to "get connected."

As you know, I was the very first to go to and graduate from college in our entire family, and you are the first child in your generation to go to college. I am so proud of you! The changes in this family continue to happen. I remember when you were having issues with your sorority sisters, and you sent me a text saying, "Mom, thank you for teaching me to live in my light." My heart was full. The work I had done on myself for so many years was paying off.

You and Josie have grown up encouraged to believe in yourselves, to love yourselves. You've learned not only how to set boundaries but also to follow them based on your self-worth.

I did it! I actually did it! I created a different environment for you girls to thrive. At times, when I look at you girls and see the opportunities you have been given, it makes me a bit sad for the little girl in me who didn't have that life. But then I remind myself, if it weren't for my inner child's upbringing, I wouldn't have had the drive, the dedication, the pure willpower to create a different foundation. We have shaped a new way of life that will carry on for generations to come.

Because of the environment I wanted to change, I found my purpose: to share the tools and possibility of the grand abundance that we are all designed for. While doing that, I have been able to change the environment for both you and Josie. I have since learned to embrace my upbringing. It has made me into the woman I am today, for which I am grateful.

I've learned to live in my light and self-worth, which has ultimately helped you girls to live in yours. As a mother, that is the greatest gift I could ever give to you girls. My heart is full.

Roxy Feller • My Dearest Jessica

Roxy Feller is a transitional coach and motivation speaker who assists others in finding the energy and focus needed to get the results they want in life. She lives in Boise, Idaho, with her two daughters. As a certified life coach, she guides individuals, professionals, entrepreneurs, and small business owners to a fulfilling, well-rounded life through the process of self-realization. With her background, training, and experience, she supports her clients as they learn and develop processes that lead them to more fulfilling and purposeful lives. She has empowered individuals and companies through one-on-one life and business coaching, keynote speaking, and group coaching.

I am gifting a one-hour coaching call with me! Let's find the magic together.

www.roxyfeller.com
www.facebook.com/roxy.eddy.3
www.instagram.com/RoxyFeller/
www.youtube.com/channel/UC4iFVefcaBX35LvHIH4YflA

Precious Smith

From the Escape House to the Forever House

It has been an interesting experience, moving from my escape house to my forever house! I have so many emotions about this journey. In May 2018, I moved to "the escape house." I was running away from a toxic situation. Losing the person I thought at the time was the love of my life, I was devastated! I don't believe I've ever been so rudely dumped and emotionally displaced.

My daughters and I packed what we could and removed ourselves from that place. All we had was love and understanding. My daughters knew that I loved them, and they understood that some days Mom was depressed and could not get out of bed. They respected my vulnerability and helped me so much with the transition. The girls were my only reason for being able to tolerate myself on many days. Those young ladies will never know how they saved my life. They helped nurture me in so many ways, just as I have nurtured and loved them!

My girls and I turned the escape house into a place of comfort. It was small and cozy, separated by floors, each of us having our own floor. It was built for individuals who need their own space. It was new for all of us.

Then I decided to write a blog. FindingMyselfat40.com was my saving grace. In the beginning it was all about exposing all the bad things that people had done to me. I spent countless days obsessing over how badly

I had been treated. I focused initially on learning to discern what were my own feelings, versus the pretend-feelings I fabricated to avoid having my real feelings hurt. Then it evolved into the things that I had allowed to destroy my self-value, those feelings of *not being enough, of primarily feeling like I was not worth a person's time and energy.*

I remember wondering why I was not worthy of being genuinely loved. I recall feeling as if the only people who could love me unconditionally were my children. Then the remarkable happened. I began to find myself in my writing. First, I examined my self-respect. It was therapeutically helpful and allowed me to really look at where and who I was, and where and who I was not! I was able to set goals, preferences, and boundaries. I was getting to know me for the first time in my adult life. It was, and is still, one of the hardest things I have ever done! I realized that I had been living my life based on "the table that was set before me." I had fallen victim to the ultimate crime of not knowing that I was worthy of being loved, which prevented me from being able to give my love to others in a free fashion, a fashion of my choosing.

I created a plan. It detailed how I would take three hundred and sixty-five days to examine myself and my life. That plan did not include any actual dating relationships. It was just me for me. I did not need anyone else! I had determined that I was an island, and that was just fine with me. All initial conversations with women included a conversation about how I was in a healing phase and only wanted to meet friends. I video dated. I joined a few social media groups. I got dressed up a few times and took some pictures. After attending a themed party, I posted a set of cute selfies. I posted them on Sunday and received many messages and compliments on the pictures and outfit. The outfit was totally outside my comfort zone. Part of finding me was finding clothes that made me comfortable. Now I realize that to be me I had to be me at one with the clothes that I wear. I really enjoy varieties in clothing. I had to learn and decide to bring all of me to every table, to have a presence at the table. So I posted!

The next day this beautiful soul of a human slid into my inbox. She was smooth from the initial conversation. I assumed she was a stranger. She asked if we could have a virtual date. I thought it was cute and agreed. I have gone on virtual dates before and did not expect it to go anywhere, but I agreed to the conversation. We had amazing chemistry even over video and telephone. During the video date I began to feel as if I had met her before and probed about her whereabouts sixteen years ago. Who remembers their whereabouts for that long? Apparently, I do, and finally, so did she.

Initially, I suppose, due to the trauma that she was experiencing, she had a harder time placing how we met. Lo and behold, she and I had met sixteen years ago in Birmingham, Alabama. That beautiful woman had not aged at all. Neither of us were from Birmingham. She was in town to see another person, and I was there following the wrong type of individuals. It was so odd. She ended up at my home, not feeling well. I nursed her back to health. I love home remedies. I believe a hot toddy will cure anything that ails you!

Out of all the people who I could have met again, the Universe dropped this amazing woman into my life twice. We have never dated, but she did come to visit for a few days. We talked on video chat and the telephone for about a month. We grew tired of just talking and reacquainting ourselves, so we decided to dip out and elope. We had to put a ring on it! Keep in mind that we had only seen each other for a few days before we decided to commit to *as long as we are both happy*. We didn't tell our families or outside friends. We did what was best for us.

We did what we wanted to do! By not being susceptible to the norms of society, we saved some money, and continued to save for a year. For example, instead of a large wedding burden, we put what we would have spent into savings. We wanted a home and decided to buy the homestead property that we found. It was the last property that we saw. We laughed all the way to view the property. It was different from everything we had done in the past. It was in an all-white neighborhood, and the property was bigger than any yard either of us had owned. My youngest daughter viewed it with us. She spent her time on a tree swing in the front and side yards. She was at peace. It was the most beautiful situation. She was able to freely be a child. There was space for her to run and play. The wife and I were convinced that this would be our home! We faced discrimination and adversity at every turn buying our home; however, as we are both very stubborn Aquariuses, we refused to be told that we could not have the home that we were able to secure financially.

We have brought diversity into a neighborhood where none existed. We became the only Black people in our neighborhood, and that will have to be alright with the neighbors. We have been in our home for about six months now, and even though it is not perfect, it is ours. We have everything we need and want. It is perfect to us! It is perfectly imperfect for our family.

This new relationship and the space we all occupied allowed me to open up to myself. I cried. I have been emotionally distraught. I have been in a serious relationship with myself, and at some point I did not like the person that I had allowed myself to become. I changed that girl in the mirror. I made a promise to myself to feel every emotion that came *to me, from me*. I learned to utilize "I" statements. It does sound a bit silly. It is only one letter. Yet, for me, using "I" was hard. I am still working on my own accountability to myself and my daughters.

I now recognize the many trauma responses that were undermining my happiness. They were the reason I stayed in a victim's mentality. I could not make a mistake or an error. I could not be anything less than perfect. I would avoid accountability by giving others the power of making me recant what I was saying.

Now that I am processing it, writing this chapter, it feels very similar to when kids get into trouble with adults. Both my daughters seem to have picked up that negative characterization as well. I decided from here forward, we are all accountable for ourselves and will use "I" statements when expressing feelings. Everyone in our home will be taking accountability for their actions. In this way, we will build and sustain our forever relationships, working on breaking generational curses within our family. Those curses stop when one person takes accountability for their actions. Then it creates a ripple effect for everyone else, now and in future generations. It is hard. It is uncomfortable. It is necessary. That is how we change the path of history—one small, accountable act at a time.

Precious Smith • From the Escape House to the Forever House

Precious Smith is a Black lesbian, wife, mother, activist, advocate, teacher, sister, daughter, and friend! She carries all those titles proudly and with adoration for every person who is a part of her human experience. She has been a teacher for eight years and a homeowner for less than a year. She teaches at a middle school in a very family-oriented neighborhood. The children she teaches, including her two daughters, are the essence of why and who she is. They have inspired her to be the best version of herself. Her amazing wife's name is Stephanie, and she has been exceptional in helping Precious realize she is more than enough! No matter how many times she was told she was enough, it didn't matter until Stephanie's actions helped her realize that she truly is *enough*. Now she teaches children to genuinely be who they are, and to authentically, unapologetically be who they are now and always.

www.findingmyselfat40.com/
www.facebook.com/precious.smith/
www.pandshomestead.com/

Kaylee House

Forgiveness and Healing

I was fourteen, on the bus on my way home from school, and totally excited. My mom had told me she'd picked up some hair dye to do my hair when I got home. Once home, I rushed into the house and put my stuff in my bedroom. Then I heard my brother, who had arrived home right before I did, yelling frantically.

I ran into my mom's bathroom. The hair dye my mom had gotten for me was sitting on the counter. Then I saw my brother trying to pull my unresponsive mother from an empty, dry bathtub. My heart sank. I was terrified, and seeing my brother so distraught really made me feel helpless. He was already on the phone with 911 telling them our address. I got in the tub to help pull her out but was unsuccessful. I was worried about strangers coming to take my naked mom away from us. I tried dressing her to save her dignity, then called my grandmother to come help.

My brother and I were lost, scared, and utterly confused. The medics rushed in, pulled her out and began working on her immediately. All I could do was ask if she would be alright, and they responded with just as much uncertainty as my brother and I were feeling.

They told me to search our pill cabinets to find any prescription medication. I hadn't acknowledged the effect of drugs or pills because that part of my mom's life was hidden from me. Except it can't really be hidden. She had overdosed on a deadly concoction of oxy and Xanax, but miraculously woke up. She woke up scared and crying with tubes down her throat and four strangers bringing her back to life.

Looking back, I realized addiction was not new to me, that it had been there for years. I thought back to all of the dinners when my mom would fall asleep, fall into her food, actually passed out. I watched her sleep years away, or that's how it felt. If she was sober and awake, she was still struggling. She tried to be a parent. I got so used to it, I just assumed that's how my mom was. Seeing other friends' moms was almost disheartening because I was so jealous. I could see how hard my mom tried, but each time she succumbed to alcohol.

My mom was in active addiction until a little over a year ago. I felt robbed of my entire teenage years and early adulthood. It felt more like I had to be her mom. I would come into her room on nights she was really messed up and lay with her to make sure she kept breathing. I would panic on nights I no longer lived with her, knowing what my sister would be seeing.

So I created a routine. I would get off work and take them pizza or sneak a little money in my mom's drawers and just check on things. My mom hardly seemed recognizable, and no one could talk sense to her. She'd been to rehabs, meetings, anything in between. She would be sober, then relapse, and it would crush me. I became bitter and angry at everything and everyone.

My approach was to deal with it on my own. I rarely reached out for help even when I really needed it. I didn't want to talk about it. I just wanted my mom to be normal. I would call my dad at all hours of the night, crying, asking him, "How can she do this to us?" As I grew older, I started to realize that she didn't want to be stuck in that place forever either. She was hurting. It was so hard to watch because I couldn't help, which made it difficult to not grow anxious and bitter at life.

I began looking for comfort and healing everywhere, but I couldn't find it until I truly forgave her. Even after my mom got sober and changed her life, I couldn't stop feeling the hurt. I would think about how she is free from that part of her life, that she's moved on from it, but I'm left with the wounds from trauma.

Then I learned the most important truth: I need to let go of it too. I hurt for my younger self and how she felt. I want to hug her and tell her everything is going to be OK. I realize now that part of the healing of my younger self comes with helping others who have to struggle with the same things. I can tell them all the things I was desperate to hear, and I can make them at least feel heard and understood. I have also learned to never let addiction become a part of my life again.

I have forgiven my mom. Forgiveness can heal a very heavy heart, and I am so happy I was there to watch my mom become sober. I've gotten to watch her be a mother, a partner, a daughter, a friend, and a sister, and she's with us to watch all her children do the same. As I move on from that part of my life, I take away the lessons and mistakes from my twenty-four trips around the sun knowing that I get to teach others and help others based on my experience. I get to carry on all I've learned, and for that I am thankful. I've learned to forgive people for unthinkable things, and I've even learned to forgive myself. Until you let go of the burden of anger, you cannot truly heal yourself.

I hope my mom forgives herself too. Forgiving and letting go has paved a pathway for me to journey into my inner self-love and all the hopeful opportunities I know are coming my way. Now I look forward to a beautiful future, taking what I've learned from my past and continuing to grow.

Kaylee House • Forgiveness and Healing

Kaylee House was born and raised in Oklahoma. She has no children of her own but is a full-time nanny. Caring for people has always been her passion. Kaylee loves to travel and to spend quality time with people she loves. Her future plans are to get involved with an organization to help fight addiction and to work with families who have dealt with or suffer from addiction. She is excited to grow and see where life takes her.

kayleekhouse@gmail.com

Julia Harriet

The Day After

"And once the storm is over, you won't remember how you made it through, how you managed to survive. You won't even be sure, whether the storm is really over. But one thing is certain. When you come out of the storm, you won't be the same person who walked in. That's what this storm's all about."
– Haruki Murakami, *Kafka on the Shore*

I fumbled, trying to grab my ringing phone off the crowded kitchen counter. I was prepping meatballs for dinner, and my hands were slippery with hamburger, egg, and cracker crumbs. Reaching for the phone, I felt something come over me, as if a storm had penetrated my kitchen, blowing into the hollows of my heart. I knew I had to answer.

I wiped the pink flesh onto my jeans and picked up the phone. "Hi, Dad."

"Julia, it's over. Your mom's gone. She's gone."

My dad's words were clipped. I swear I could hear the storm in my kitchen thrashing around him, blowing in the hollows of his heart as well.

I smelled raw meat on my fingertips just as gut-wrenching pain flooded my chest and mind. I swallowed. My tongue caught on the back of my dry throat, causing me to choke and cough.

My mother had been in hospice care for the past two months. I'd played this moment over in my mind several times, imagining this call. Nothing could have prepared me for the piercing sorrow of my mother's passing, the anguish churning through my veins, the sound of my scream reverberating between my ears. Did I scream out loud? Or was it just my cough?

Shit, I had forgotten I was still on the phone with my father.

"Dad, are you OK? Oh fuck. What can I do for you?"

My dad had been by my mother's side nonstop, barely eating, sleeping, or bathing since she slipped into a catatonic slumber over three weeks before. He refused my efforts to relieve him, even momentarily, though all I wanted was to protect both my parents from this symbiotic slide into an abyss.

"I need you to take care of yourself and the kids. I'll come up there as soon as I get things settled with your mom and the house."

"OK. We will figure this out together. I love you so much, Dad."

He hung up first. I looked at my dinner preparations with disgust and staggered out into the living room. My kids would be coming home from school soon. I had no idea how to handle this or, for that matter, my ricocheting emotions.

Looking desperately out the window, my eyes fell on the one-hundred-year-old lighthouse. A year ago, we had moved from the city to become the new keepers of the Point Robinson Lighthouse on a little island in Washington. It wasn't lost on me that I happened to be just seventy-five feet from a powerful beacon of safety and hope as an emotional hurricane churned inside of me. I would never be the same.

It was time to walk up to the bus stop. My children understood that grandma was very sick, but neither had ever lost someone this close to them. My mom was the type to get down and play when we came for a visit, and no one read a bedtime story like Grandma wrapped in her fuzzy gray bathrobe.

As the bus rumbled over the hill, air wafted across my hot face. I was about to deliver horrible news to my children, and I had no words to coat the bitterness. The bus stopped, and the door opened. Bounding into my arms, two enchanted beings wrapped themselves around me. In the profound comfort of their embrace, my sorrow broke into a torrent of tears.

"Mama, what's wrong?" my daughter asked. "Oh Mama, tell us!"

"Grandma left us today. She passed away this afternoon." Standing on the side of the road, my children fiercely kept their arms around me. "I love you both so much." Looking down into their soft stares of confusion, I felt such loss, thinking nothing would ever be the same again.

"Mama, will we ever see Grandma again?" my son asked.

"No, honey. But Grandma will always be with you. Right here." I touched my son's heart, and he smiled, placing his small hand over mine.

"Her love for you both never goes away."

"But what about Grandpa?" my daughter asked.

My oldest knew that Grandpa wasn't doing well either. He looked as sickly as my mother did the last time we saw them.

"Grandpa is going to come here and stay with us so we can figure things out together."

My children looked at each other in bewilderment. It was a lot to take in.

"All I know is that Grandpa's gonna need a lot of hugs. And help."

Hand in hand, we slowly started walking. My legs were weak and trembling. Though my children stood below my shoulders, I could feel them actively bracing me.

From behind an alder tree, the lighthouse appeared. Peeking through the skeletal branches, the eye of light blinked on and off as though to say, *I see you, Julia. I see you.* I wasn't sure I wanted to be seen, but I acknowledged that there was no way to hide.

"Mama, what's for dinner?" That was my son's favorite question. It felt reassuringly normal.

I remembered my meatballs with disgust. "Mac and cheese."

We settled back in our humble caretaker's quarters, and it hit me. *Now what do I do?* Life was happening, just like the tide rising outside my door. Nothing I could do to change it.

Following our usual evening routine, it was time to tuck my children into their bunks. Normally, I reveled in this moment, the transition from mothering to me-time. But after saying goodnight, I was alone, clutched by unfamiliar, aching grief.

I paced from the living room to the kitchen and back again. The knot of sorrow could not be contained. Much like the outcry when birthing, the song of death is unstoppable. Tears turned to sobs, and sobs turned to moans as I folded onto the kitchen floor. What emerged from my soul was the primal wail of mourning.

I knew my children could hear me, but I couldn't stop. I shivered, concerned about exposing my grief to their young hearts, but knew there was no shielding myself or others from the truth. The loss overwhelmed me. I was no longer a woman, a daughter, or a mother. I was a human in a violent battle with mortality.

Looking out the single-pane windows of the caretaker's cottage, I reminded my lungs to breathe in, out. Hours passed, but I didn't move from the corner of the kitchen floor. When I shut my eyes, my mother appeared. She looked concerned, reminiscent of a time when I had fallen off my bike and arrived home with bloody knees. She held me, the little ball of sadness that I was.

I must have slipped into a form of slumber because when I awoke, the morning's first glow was at the crest of the lighthouse. I quietly entered my kids' room, sitting first on my son's bed to wake him for school.

"Mama," he said softly. "I heard you being very sad last night. Do you need a hug?"

"Yes, I do. I hope I didn't scare you. I was really missing my mom last night."

At this point, both my children were awake. *We had made it to the day after.*

My son put his hand on my cheek. "My heart can hold your hurting heart, Mama."

"Thank you, honey. My heart is very grateful for you both."

I stood up and noticed a commotion outside. A group of visitors had gathered and were pointing out into the water. Straining my puffy eyes to see, I spotted a black dorsal fin rising up out of the gray water. It was the orcas.

"Oh my goodness, kids! The orcas are here. Come quick!"

We ran to the window to discover five majestic whales passing right in front of our house. Known locally as the J Pod, they were a family of resident orcas traveling south less than twenty feet from the beach.

"Oh wow! Let's get closer!" My son flew out the door and scrambled down the driftwood toward the waterline.

The whales slid effortlessly in and out of the water, like pieces of silk being woven together.

"Look! I can see Grandma's spirit riding on the back of the one in the middle! Can you see her out there too, Mama?"

As I focused, the orca breached into the air, affirming a good time was being had by all.

"Yes! I do see her, sweetie! She even got the whale to do a trick for you!"

A hearty cheer rang out among the growing crowd of spectators. Our mouths were agape in awe of this amazing experience. My heart was beating wildly, and I felt suspended in wonder.

In this magical moment, standing on the beach with wild orcas breaching, I experienced a profound wave of relief. The pain subsided long enough for me to surface, relish the salty air, and smile as I pictured my mom passing by, free from the weight of her illness. In my mind, there we were, riding side by side on the backs of these gorgeous creatures.

"Mama, can you believe this? I think it's a sign that everyone will be OK again."

"Yes, I do too. They are messengers of hope, aren't they?"

"Hope will heal our hearts."

"That and a whole lot of hugs."

Julia Harriet is a #1 international best-selling author, an inspirational speaker, and a builder who has been working in construction for over six years on Vashon Island, Washington. After earning her MIT, she spent a decade teaching everything from preschool to high school art. Julia left the field of education to once again become a student at age thirty-five when she started a carpentry apprenticeship. She successfully built her own home for her family and enjoys supporting others in DIY home-improvement projects. Julia also volunteers for a nonprofit in her community, Project Dove, which works to support victims of domestic and interpersonal violence. Julia's memoir, *Under Construction: Healing Trauma While Building My Dream*, became a #1 international bestseller in four countries in 2021 and a #1 bestseller in nine categories, including new release in Happiness. Julia considers herself to be everyone's builder buddy and loves to support women in constructing their dreams, no matter what obstacles appear in the way.

She welcomes all inquiry @ juliaharriet.com

www.facebook.com/juliaharriet
www.instagram.com/julia.harriet.builds/
www.linkedin.com/in/juliaharriet
www.youtube.com/user/jhander333/featured

Kenya Evelyn

The Bridge

I never felt that I fit in. I desperately wanted to. I did everything I thought I needed to do to be accepted by my mom, my church, and my friends. I knew my life was big; I just didn't know that it was OK for me to be big. Nobody talked to me about greatness, leadership, big dreams, big energy, big personality. And no one mentioned having a big mission.

I grew up in Brazil in a single-family home. My mom worked three jobs while my grandmother cared for me and my sister. I have always been an artist, a lover of people and nature. I can love with passion *just because*. When I was little, everyone seemed to love me, but as soon as I became a teenager, I could no longer hug and kiss people just because I loved them or because I felt that they needed me. I was labeled "easy" and other names. I quickly noticed that I was praised for how much I did. So I kept doing more and "helping" others that way. I started to close my heart. Not having a dad made it even harder.

I remember being lost in time and space because of a sunset or the feel of the sand under my feet. I didn't know that I was an empath and a lightworker. I work with others to help them wake up, find their light, and understand their energy. I didn't know about my gifts. I was the girl who could sing. I accepted as many invitations to perform as I could because it meant making people happy, feeling close to God, and coming home with my entire body vibrating, fully alive.

Otherwise, I played small. I thought I was accustomed to it, but I was cringing inside. I asked, "Is this life? Is this it?" Everyone seemed to be OK with it. But I was dying inside.

My mom left me in Brazil in a boarding school when I was thirteen. My heart broke. I didn't want to be without her. I would later learn that her heart broke too. She continued to work even harder to make sure that my sister and I had a college education.

After finishing my music therapy bachelor's degree, I went to be with my mom. Little did I know that healing, awakening, and discovery were about to take place.

What allowed this healing, awakening, and discovery? I finally stopped believing that if I shined too bright, my light would stop others from shining their light. I now know and tell you with confidence that is one hundred percent wrong. As I own my power, my light, and my story, I give others physical evidence of what is possible.

We are the only ones that can shut us down or fire us up. I believe our soul knows who we are and what we are meant to be, do, and have. But we must listen to the calling. What is it?

What if there is nothing more for us to "figure out" or "do"? What if we heard our soul calling for us to be, to laugh more, to fill our being?

When you are in your authentic state of being, everything you do carries your aligned vibration, your unique signature of God-given designed frequency.

The process of deconditioning from compulsive *doing* to *being* is a journey that starts with a decision. Your arrival is preset so you feel great about yourself, simply by being you, doing absolutely nothing to earn your value. You are valuable, you are divine light, you are love and loved by being you.

I came out of a rich season of my life—a season of twelve years of homeschooling three kids and being a stay-at-home mom—ready for the new chapter that was knocking on my door. On this particular day, I was overcome with joy and gratitude for having the courage to let go and trust the seeds I had planted in my kids so they would blossom in the real world. I was exhausted from living in a state of doing, subconsciously repeating the pattern of doing more to obtain more worth, doing more to receive more love.

As I awakened, I learned that being and fulfillment are my birthright, that I could shed the generational layers of expectations to achieve—layers of doing instead of being. This was the greatest gift I could give to myself, my kids, and humanity.

I look around at the mess, the things that don't belong. The disorganization, the pull to keep doing and doing…there's so much to do! There's always so much to do. In the house there's so much to clean, so much to wash . . . it's all too much. It's never-ending. Yet there is a part of me that knows *doing* is an illusion. I get caught up in the frequency of "catching up" and the frequency of feeling that if I don't keep up or catch up, one task will swell into an overwhelming mountain of things.

So I ask, in which moment, at which part of my life, in which season, do I stop to *be*?

Be still and know that *I am*, to know *I am whole and complete.* There's nothing else to do. I know that I am *free*! I am free to sing, I am free to dance, I am free! All is well for me, and everyone in my life knows that nothing is missing. There is nothing broken, and there is nothing to conquer or to create.

When I am stripped down from all outside frequencies that pull me in every direction, always wanting more of me, my soul tells me, "It's all an illusion. You have always been perfect. You have always been loved. Your essence is my essence. In my divine design, you are aligned with God and you resonate light and love. You resonate with completion."

When I resonate positive vibrations, I am a *masterpiece* of love. Everything I get to do in that state is a gift that I choose to give to myself and others. All the have-to-dos are on the floor. All the must-dos are blown away like feathers in the wind.

When you see me, or others living in alignment, something inside of you resonates. You feel a new question: could this be possible for you? I am telling you, *yes*.

Coming back to your originating frequency is coming back *home*. It's turning down and turning off all outside distortion, programming, and expectations and surrendering to your divine being of wholeness. It reveals a deeper level of love. You are not just loved; you are love itself. You are not just reflecting light from above; you are light. You have godly DNA. You are designed by the hand of God.

How valuable are you? When you look in the mirror, do you see the priceless you? Suddenly there are no wrinkles or imperfections. You are loving what is, and your cells vibrate in gratitude! You are tired of doing. Let your soul scream, *I am free*! Let the spirit smile inside, shed the weight of just playing a game, a game of survival. Open to the energy resonating deep inside yourself as you move from pain to pleasure, from dullness to brilliance.

You have always known you are more, but feeling disconnected, you absorbed what others projected onto you—unsuitable projections, because they weren't yours to live.

From this place of knowing and feeling at home, aligned, everything is different. Motherhood is different. Being a woman is different. You set your kids free from passed-down generational expectations and agreements. By choice, you rise and take a stand. The dis-ease stops with you. From this place, forgiving others becomes effortless. In your mind, you now know that they were doing their best. In their way, they helped you to become you.

Imagine if you knew how to unconditionally love yourself from the get-go. How would you have set the tone differently for all the relationships to come, starting with yourself and God? To accept that God unconditionally loves you is to believe that you do not have to earn His love and that nothing can separate you from Him.

Loving yourself this much and filling your cup is the secret sauce to loving others in a way that they can receive; but first know, no one can love you more than you love yourself.

I get it that few humans have had this kind of love modeled for them. That is why it is important for the rest of us to decide to write a new story, a story of giving from a place of overflowing acceptance, of loving yourself so completely that you can't help but love others. And the people who are able to meet you at the frequency you have discovered—this subtle vibration, a language that everyone feels without using words—are the people you can choose to be among.

As I walked the bridge from doing to being, I looked back and saw not just generations but entire cultures that reward doing, overachieving, and hard-fought wealth. I choose to turn on my light and shine so bright that it guides others to find their way through doing to becoming, to being all of themselves.

Kenya Evelyn lives in Nashville, Tennessee, with her three kids and husband of seventeen years. She is passionate about God, her family, and awakening the truth of our light and the power of our being. A lifelong singer and certified music therapist, energy healer, health coach, and life coach, she calls herself an Intuitive Frequency Alchemist. She teaches others how to harmonize their energy, vibration, and frequency to achieve a life of fun, fulfillment, and purpose—what she calls *wealth*—through aligned frequency. Kenya believes in creating stronger families and supporting women who love themselves so unconditionally that everything they touch is calibrated with the frequency of abundance. She creates with ease and flow; hosts retreats and singing circles; provides one-on-one coaching; facilitates "Night of Healing WARM: Women, Accepting and Releasing Movement" and Motherhood with Ease. She invites you to reclaim your voice, find your rhythm, learn your frequencies, discover your divine design, and amplify your power through voice and movement.

www.kenyaevelyn.com

Nataliya Preiss

pHenomenal[1] Life
From Burnout to Life in Balance

If you felt like a Ferrari at the beginning of the romantic relationship, and now you feel like a pickup truck, let's take a breath and find the moment you lost your inner balance.

"When did it happen? When was the first incident, the very first time you abandoned yourself? Neglected your needs? Betrayed your inner Queen?" I asked my girlfriend, then repeated, "When did it happen? Try to remember."

We sat in a cozy cafe in sunny California. My girlfriends often reached out for advice, given the mix of my professional certifications and wisdom of two failed marriages. I would put on my "therapist hat" and offer my shoulder to cry on for another beautiful soul, and remind her about her awesomeness:

"Sweetheart, you are a Ferrari. You just forgot." I wiped the tears from my friend's face and hugged her: "You are precious. You are perfect. You are a once-in-a-lifetime cosmic event. Love yourself first."

---

1 Understanding the importance of normal pH levels in the body first requires understanding what the pH scale represents and how it affects the body's functions. Body systems require a level of both acidity and alkalinity to protect against disease and promote healing. Too much, or too little, of either can be damaging to various physical and mental activities. pH Balance: How an Unbalanced pH Affects the Body (doctorshealthpress.com, 2018).

Two years later, I found myself in the gynecologist's office. My last visit was before the lockdown two years ago.

"You missed last year's annual checkup?" Dr. K frowned at me.

"I was busy."

"Too busy for your annual checkup?"

"You don't understand. We had a product launch last year, and then we had to scale and hire more people. I am dealing with three teams in different time zones. I've been sleeping five hours for the past two years. I don't even have time to have—"

Dr. K interrupted me. "I want you to have an ultrasound and most likely a biopsy. The oncologist will explain it."

"—a facial or a massage, last time I had it…What? An oncologist?" I felt dizzy.

I visualized long hours in the office, thousands of emails, and hundreds of Zoom calls.

What if an oncologist said I had six months to live? That's all I would remember?

My last two years of life were endless stressful situations I had put myself in. For what? For some idea that I'd have a financial reward big enough to ensure a comfortable life one day. I worked as hard as a man in the man-dominated tech industry, and burned out physically to the point I lost my health, my spark, my joy.

"I am so tired!" I collapsed on my doctor's shoulder as I wiped away my tears. "I feel like a pickup truck…"

I went home, silently weeping in the back of the Uber, realizing people don't change when they see the light. Often, we only change when we feel the heat. That day I received my wake-up call. There were things I had to do, conversations I needed to have, like:

"Do you love me?"

"I do. Do you still love me?"

"Yes. But…"

"Do you feel we are not in love anymore?"

"Yes. I feel like working together killed our love."

"You are my best friend. I'll always love you."

The movers. Wrapping my furniture, taking boxes to a strange new place. I had to start over again.

How did I let it happen? When did it happen the very first time? I tried to remember. When did I start betraying myself? When did I say "yes" when I wanted to say "hell, no!" It starts with a little thing, just one. And another one. And then you don't even notice when you betray yourself in a big way.

I needed to figure out why on earth we women do that.

Falling in love. What is wrong with this sentence? Not "love," of course. It's the "falling" part. It happens to a lot of women: two people come together, and a woman usually falls. A woman tends to mold herself according to what her man wants her to be. She puts her dreams on the shelf. The "pleaser" mask that most women are conditioned to wear seems like a formula for a happy marriage, a default path many women take, not knowing it leads to self-destruction.

2021 was simultaneously the absolute best and worst year of my life, a year of extreme highs and extreme lows. It showed me that pain and pleasure can coexist simultaneously; that I can be in deep sadness while also feeling unconditional love; that I can experience deep gratitude and the righteous anger/feminine rage of Kali; that I can feel trapped and enjoy living in a hermit's state with success and burnout, depression and reverence for life, losing everything and rising like a phoenix from the ashes.

In 2021, I died and gave birth to myself multiple times. I was tested on all levels. And I am grateful for all my scars—they are my treasures.

Looking back, I see that the best gifts in life can come in the worst gift wrapping.

I realized my body was giving me hints to rest, to recharge. I ignored all the red flags. I disregarded the symptoms and minimized how I felt. I put everything and everyone first, taking even more tasks on my full plate. I did not know how to ask for help or how to delegate. I was heading full force into burning out my adrenals, whacking my hormones, and depleting my immune system.

"If you listen to your body when it whispers, you won't have to hear it scream." — Dan Millman

The ridiculous thing is that I am an educated woman with two master's degrees and a bunch of certifications in health and nutrition. I trained with the best coaches in the world. With Marisa Peer, I studied the brain, psychology, and hypnotherapy, helping people with emotional eating, owning "I am enough," getting out of toxic relationships, and finding life balance.

Coaching and educating women used to be my passion. That was exactly why I joined this tech startup—to bring nutritional awareness to every kitchen, to honor women's bodies while enjoying foods they love. I wanted to inspire a healthy relationship with food as a way to celebrate life, not escape from it.

As much knowledge as we have, we all have blind spots. I hadn't noticed when, little by little, I started moving from the things I loved to performing the tasks that killed my creative spirit. I started having dissatisfaction and suppressed resentment that I did not allow myself to feel. The unexpressed emotions stored in the body later manifest in disease.

Short calming meditations and balanced nutrition helped me survive the crazy work hours, stressful negotiations, and the hiring and training of new teams. The reality was that, working in a tech startup as an executive,

I had to wear many "hats." There was no such thing as nine-to-five office hours. I worked nonstop, and I was lucky if I squeezed a shower between the 10:00 p.m. call with Poland and the 1:00 a.m. call with India. I lived on the global schedule of my international tech teams.

After a few months of the constant pressure of deadlines, I lost my *Self As A Woman*. I became a machine that delivered results. Everything had to be under control. There was no time to feel weak, frustrated, or emotional. I shuffled my emotions under the rug to deal with them "later." Everything became "later." Later we'd have money, and later we'd enjoy life. I had a competitive "must deliver" attitude, a hustling lifestyle, and a long to-do list—the masculine way of doing business. It became unbearable. I started wondering whether there was another way of building a business empire and still having joy—the feminine way?

That thought made me realize I was not divorcing my man; I wanted to run away from *the person I had become*: the exhausted, bitchy, "strong" woman who lost her feminine magnetism. I lost my inner Queen. I lost the inner Goddess. I betrayed my light, abandoned myself, neglected my needs and my boundaries. I put business first, burning myself into depression, being out of my truth.

Most people think that it is the fall that kills. It's never the fall; it's the landing. I had to land gracefully, land with gratitude.

Gratitude meditations helped me to find joy again, helped me to follow my dreams and step into my authenticity to create a life I'd love, which meant embracing *all* of who I am, especially the parts I tried to stuff away and hide from.

If we want to feel like a Ferrari again, we have to change our lifestyle habits. From the food we eat and the thoughts we are marinated in to the self-love rituals we have each day, all of these choices reflect the level of our standards.

To me, Ferrari means having high standards. Would you put cheap oil in a luxury car?

"Ferrari" is the *Woman* in us, the feminine energy.

What we want, what we need, is to feel nourished as a well-fed Woman. I don't mean only in a physical nutrition sense, even though it starts there. I mean energetically fed, taken care of, honored. Magic happens when we can own that we do have needs, own what those needs are, and give them to ourselves. And when we can't, we ask for help.

So, I committed to the rule: "Feed the Feminine First." Fill my cup up so much that it's overflowing with joy, vibrant energy, and excitement, which is what I teach at my women-only pHenomenal retreats. I learned how to get from burnout to life in balance by releasing suppressed emotions with the help of HypnoBreathwork®, ecstatic dance, sound healing, meditations, and yummy nutrition that supports female hormones. I teach women—from high-achievers and female executives to overwhelmed moms—the practical tools to restore life balance, reignite health and happiness, and get the sparkle back. Feel. Receive. Embody. Because how alive you feel matters. Finding what brings you joy and makes you feel alive—that is what makes your life phenomenal.

What else have I learned?

I learned the magic of raw surrender. I learned to love every high and low and accept them as equally important parts of my journey. I learned the beauty of letting go and letting the Universe open my heart to endless opportunities for growth. I realized that if I wanted to experience *more*, I must surrender. I needed to let go of control. I decided to accept what comes my way, and I chose to feel it *all*.

But first I had to thrive within myself. To drop in, to show up, to love myself, and then, only then, I would be able to rise as a Woman.

"Love yourself first." This is the advice I share with every woman and girl in my life. "Stay true to yourself. Be yourself! If you try to be something different, when you go against your true nature, you will suffocate from the inside out."

I learned to be myself again.

Now, I do not pretend to be someone I am not. I embrace that I am too honest, too strong, too intense, too wild, too emotional. I am a badass and fight fiercely. I love too hard and feel too deeply. I command respect because I learned never to abandon myself. I learned not to apologize for who I am, because I understand myself. Because I am the only one who has lived my life and learned from my story. I know myself. I know who I am, what I feel, what I do, and why I do it.

So I release my partner from the obligation to make me feel complete. I lack nothing in myself. I love myself. Therefore, I allow my partner into my world to see the love in me. I don't worry about what other people think. Instead, I go within and listen. Oh yes, I listen and feel that I am perfect, just as I am right now.

I stand in my truth.

I rise and roar like a playful tigress.

I radiate love and kindness.

I surrender to joy, balance, and bliss.

And I make my life pHenomenal.

I am a Woman. This is my superpower.

What is yours?

Even though Nataliya Preiss built a multi-million dollar company, Nataliya believes she is not just a businesswoman but a Spiritual Entrepreneur. Nataliya is Female Leadership Mentor, HypnoBreathwork®, and Happy Balance Coach who weaves together unique teachings and healing experiences for women to awaken, embody and express their brilliance.

Nataliya is a great model for women who are kicking ass but struggling to retain or better express their Feminine. As a result of her own healing journey, Nataliya approaches the body functionally, understanding that sickness, disease, and suffering are not separate from but directly linked to emotions stored in our bodies. At exclusive retreats for women, Nataliya holds tender space for deep journeys from past traumas into the joy and ecstasy that a HypnoBreathwork® practice provides while specializing in food as medicine, detox, and working intuitively to help women gain direction, healing, and empowerment—mind, body, and spirit.

Exclusive retreats for women: www.PHretreats.com
www.instagram.com/be.phenomenal/

The story above is an excerpt from the upcoming book "pHenomenal Life. From Burnout to Life in Balance," you can pre-order at www.ph-book.com

Amy Joy

The Power of Perspective

What separates a victim from a victor?

For me, being a victim or a victor depends on my perspective. It's all in how I see things. There is great power in being able to focus one's perspective on positive outcomes, even when surrounded by nothing but negatives.

One of the most unbelievable examples of the power of perspective is my story about Dani. My best friend Daniela (Dani) was stabbed nine times. Nine times. Life happened for her. For both of us that day.

She called while I was in a meeting with my brother. I heard her words, but my mind couldn't compute what she said. She told me again in a weak voice, "I've been stabbed."

My mind and body burst into action. I told my brother, "Dani's been stabbed" and ran to my car holding the phone in my hand and Dani in my heart.

"Dani, I'm on my way, stay with me on the phone." Coincidentally, I was right outside the best hospital in town. I ran into the lobby and handed the phone to the attendant to get Dani's address. I ran back to my car, and the ambulance and I tore off to her house at the same time.

On the way, I learned her attacker was gone. He had left Dani and her daughter, Sophia, alone in the house, and Sophia was not hurt. I knew Dani and I had to keep talking so I could keep her conscious.

"There's blood everywhere," she whispered.

"Put pressure on the wound," I reminded her, assuming she had been stabbed once.

"I can't."

I didn't understand. "What do you mean?"

"I don't have the strength."

Again, I asked her, "What do you mean?"

She answered, "Because they are all over."

With those words, the blood drained from my face. I was flying down the road, casting forgiveness and understanding into the air as I cut people off and raced past them. I kept breathing deeply.

"Breathe with me, Dani." I kept telling myself she would be OK. I was calling on Source to please save her.

"I'm cold." Her voice was weaker with every word.

I knew this was a bad sign. "OK, Dani, open your mind, put yourself into a beautiful hot tub of super perfect warm water cascading around you. Can you do that? Feel the warm water. I'm almost there. Hold on!"

I screeched to a halt outside her door right behind the ambulance and ran inside. I found her lying on the kitchen floor, blood everywhere, people everywhere. She had called her husband, and he had called others. He was talking to the police. The paramedics went into action.

I stepped around the puddles of blood to be at her head. I looked into her terrified eyes and told her, "You're going to be OK. Help is here."

The paramedics bandaged her up the best they could without knowing how many times she had been stabbed. They asked which hospital they should take her to. I looked into their eyes and said, "To the very best one." Despite a possible closer hospital, I intuitively knew that to save her would require the best doctors and equipment.

Her husband asked me to go in the ambulance with her. At first I didn't understand why, but then it sunk in. I was not just her best friend; I was her life coach. Of course I needed to be with her right now! I climbed into the ambulance, shoved a foot under each set of legs and wheels, and lifted her head in my hands. I held her as the ambulance flew down the highway, sirens blaring. I looked down into her big brown puppy-dog eyes, and I could see how scared she was.

An overwhelming wave of fear passed over me. I wanted to puke. I wanted to cry. I wanted to collapse. I was terrified I would lose my best friend. I knew she had a very small chance for survival, maybe 20 to 30 percent. I'd seen too much of this in New Guinea working there as a missionary, dealing with trauma emergencies. I had this overwhelming fear that was almost crippling, but then . . . I remembered my training and my teachings.

I remembered the phrase that I learned from my amazing mentor, Tony Robbins. Life is happening for you. Not to you. *Life is happening for you, not to you, Amy.*

I completed the phrase in my own way. "Life is happening *for* me, and *everything* is here to help me." I then experienced a sudden, massive realization: "If life is happening for me and I'm no more special than anybody else on the planet, then that means life is also happening for Dani, and she just got stabbed nine times! Holy shit!"

I had been coaching her for months and knew Dani had adopted this philosophy. But we had no idea we were preparing ourselves for one of the biggest challenges of our lives!

In that moment of realization, I was able to look down at her and say, "You've got this, girl. Everything is working out. Look, you're in an ambulance. You are not alone on the floor. We are in an ambulance. We are getting help. They know what they're doing. We will make it to the hospital. Every cell in your body is working for you, right now. Your blood is clotting. It is keeping you from bleeding out. You are healing right now. Here's what we're going to do. When you get through this, we're going to do so many amazing things, and we're going to travel. Where do you want to go? You want to go to New York, right?"

She sort of nodded. I said, "OK, let's go to New York. We'll go to New York and we'll see snow." She had never seen snow, and I knew she really wanted to. "We'll see the lights at Christmas; we're going to have that experience together someday. And you're going to see Sophia grow up! Sophie needs you." I prayed to The Divine for help and kept encouraging her the best I could. I said, "Honey, you're gonna do great, you're gonna be a bright, shining light of how *not* to be a victim!"

When we got to the hospital and she was safely in the doctors' capable hands, I allowed myself to lose my shit. For two minutes, I fell into a heap in my brother's arms, who had gone from our meeting to the hospital next door. I cried it out! Then I shook it off and did what I had to do to be the friend she needed at that moment—someone to hold, send, and believe all the positive messages that would help her.

She died twice on the table. They took her kidney and her spleen. Her kidney was completely obliterated from being stabbed so many times.

The next day, her vitals were completely stable. It was a miracle! I looked at the doctors' faces; they could not believe it. They said she would be in the hospital for one to two months. She ended up staying for a week. One week! How? Because she believed that life was happening *for* her, and everything was here *to help her*. She repeated that over and over until she left that hospital one week later.

This isn't a story about the person who stabbed her, so I'm not going to get into those details. This is a story about powerful healing energy, a story about perspective.

Dani is a bright, shiny example of how not to be a victim. The forensic doctor at the trial said words I will never forget: "There's only one reason Dani is alive, and that's because she willed herself to be so."

Dani and I were able to get through this very challenging time because each of us has the individual philosophy and belief system that *Life is Happening For Me, and Everything is Here to Help Me.*. Period.

It's not a sometimes philosophy. It isn't something that comes and goes, depending on the circumstances. This is an all the time, in every circumstance belief. Without it, I can become a victim and believe life is out to get me. With it, I am a victor with the power of my mind.

Everything can be put into this perspective. It's a lot more fun to believe that life is happening for me and that everything is here to help me. I know that when I look for the gifts of "everything is here to help me," I will find them!

The negative is available to each of us at any time, and so is the positive. Victim or victor? It is a matter of perspective. In this story, Dani and I chose the power of our perspectives. Life is happening for us. I hope that you will choose the perspective that brings the sun and allows you to shine, like we did!

Amy Joy is a mentor, coach, and healer at Amy Joy Coaching, and owner of Upaya Healing Center, where people come to work on their mind, body, and soul. She is the author of the book *Get Your Shit Together: How to go from Fear to Freedom*, launching September 2022. She is a sacred Kambo facilitator, Reiki master, and is certified in sound, instant miracle, and crystal healing. Amy worked four years as a missionary in the jungles of Papua New Guinea. She has been a teacher's aide for special needs children, and a camp counselor. Amy is a single mother of two sons by birth plus another son by unofficial adoption. She escaped an abusive marriage, started over in a foreign country, and is thriving and living her best life. Amy loves people and is passionate about helping and inspiring them to live extraordinary lives.

www.amyjoy360.com/

Vanessa Tynes-Jass

The First Dark Night

It was the first dark night of many. I'd convinced myself there was only one option left. It was a cold and rainy night in November when I was summoned from the park bench and told I could stay in their house as long as I did as the other girls did. When the girls found out I was going with them, they were a lot nicer and began revealing their truths to me.

The next day, I was taken to the drugstore for supplies. As we walked through Shoppers Drug Mart, the other girls were with me. He stayed in the car to avoid being noticed by onlookers. Why would a middle-aged man be with a group of young girls buying these types of supplies? The shopping cart was filled with dark-colored makeup, eyeliner, sponges, lipstick, pantyhose, boxes and boxes of condoms, and douches.

God knows I had no idea what those were at the time! I picked up the box and asked, "What is this?" Someone answered, "It's a douche." That was not helpful. Each time we put something in the basket, I was told what it was for. The details didn't resonate with me until later. It was clear to me they all knew what they were doing, so it was best that I just follow their instructions.

They said, "Buy whatever you think you need!" I was a teenager in a drugstore, who basically wore the same undergarments for a week because I didn't have a spot to wash them. Now here I am with other girls being permitted to buy whatever I needed. I think I just wanted some candy! I was finally able to get some deodorant, toothpaste, hair spray, hair gel, shampoo and conditioner, and my own new toothbrush. Notwithstanding my excitement at the new goodies I had in the bag, I was sick to my stomach most of the day with anxiety about not knowing what was in store for me.

While she did my makeup and hair that evening, Tonia, who was the most outspoken, told me the rules, told me what to say and what not to say. She also told me how to watch out for the police, and what not to do if the police picked me up. She told me that the police who handle the "stroll" are called "morality police," and that we can be charged with "communicating for the purpose of prostitution." She told me that the undercover officers will come by and ask you questions and wait for you to incriminate yourself. She told me that they are not allowed to touch you, so it's best just to ask them to touch your chest, or your breast, skin to skin. She said if they refuse to do that, the next test was for them to show you their penis. She assured me that no officer had revealed his penis to a girl on the street.

"Police?" When she gave me that advice, I was terrified. How would I keep myself from being charged? I knew at that moment that my future would not happen if I had a criminal record. Looking back, I am not surprised that my inner soul knew I had a future ahead of me and that this was a moment of survival. This thought was astonishing. I remember the makeup being caked on my face, and I remember thinking it was a lot of makeup. I wasn't used to using a lot, if any, makeup. My hair was like a helmet and didn't move when Tonia was finished.

I had a litany of questions racing through my mind but no voice to speak them aloud. As we all squeezed into the back seat, he put on music and seemed to be in a happy mood. He turned it up, and everyone was smiling and laughing around me. I stared out the window as we drove.

It was ten o'clock at night. Driving over the bridge into the sister city of Halifax, I watched the lights on the bridge pass by and wondered how I could get out of this, if I would be able to back out of it. I wondered what would happen when we got there. I was never really told what I would be doing and where. I was told the rules—don't speak to police, dress this way, do your makeup this way, and use two condoms—but nothing about standing on the street, or going into alleys, or getting in cars, or any other details that one may want to know before such an undertaking. I just did not know what to expect. They said it would be easy, just like doing it with my boyfriend, but using two condoms and with no kissing. That was all the information I was given, which clearly was not enough to prepare me for the hell I was about to experience.

During that drive, he must have noticed the look of fear on my face, because he started talking to me directly about foolishness in an attempt to make me relax or laugh, or to relate to the song that was on. He made jokes with me about music, or other things that would make the girls laugh. Or he would sing and be charming with the girls.

When we got to the location, all the girls got out except me. I was scared but was soon forced out of the car and onto the street with the other girls. Attempting to hide from potential customers, I was spotted by a man. Someone negotiated a price for me, and I went with this stranger. The man was about my height, Middle Eastern and heavyset, probably forty years old. He immediately took his clothes off. I did not. As he stretched out on the bed with his socks still on, I sat on the side and reconciled my thoughts from "what the fuck am I doing?" to "just do it and get it over with, there's no other choice." I proceeded to do the deed. No kissing. Easy. Just turn your head as he tries. When he got on top of me, his weight took my breath away. It felt like a world was on my chest. I suddenly remembered another time in the not too distant past when I had to just lay there, exit my body, and pretend I was somewhere else and count the seconds, smell the breath on the side of my neck, the beads of sweat dripping on my skin, making my skin crawl with every drop.

What was different from this time? Not much, except I was in a beautiful hotel room for the first time in the big city of Halifax. What a great memory. I turned my head to the side and waited for him to finish. I remember looking at his hairy shoulder and just counting slowly in my mind. One, two, three, four, five, six . . . then my light left my body, just like the end of a sunset. I couldn't feel. I was numb. It didn't hurt physically. What did hurt was my heart. I wanted to cry, and I wanted to run. I wanted to do a lot in reaction to that act, but I just couldn't. I had to hold it in.

I held it in for many dark nights after that first one. I kept the light out of my heart when my roommate was murdered. I kept the light out of my heart when I was finally able to escape, and kept it snuffed out of my soul during the best moments in my life. I let a glimmer of my light out when my children were born. My kids are my world, but they were not enough to let all my light shine. My soul was as dark as the secret that I held through everything. I held the secret of my time being trafficked on the streets until just a few years ago. I became a successful lawyer and still kept that darkness with me every day, until my soul advised me that it was time to finally let my light shine.

In my darkest moment, I knew that when I let that secret out to the world, it would reveal an incredible story of survival, resilience, bravery, and strength. When I was able to finally tell my secret, I was shocked at the outpouring of love, support, and admiration that people gave me. I never knew my story would be inspirational to others. I always thought of it as my shame. It turned out that my darkness was my light; it was my sun. It was the thing that protected and defined me, allowing me to become the woman I am today.

Vanessa Tynes-Jass, BA, LLB, is the founder of Survivors Unleashed International. Vanessa is the principal lawyer of two law practices in the Greater Toronto Area. She is also a seasoned entrepreneur of over twenty years and a lawyer coach. As a survivor of domestic sex trafficking, she has firsthand knowledge and experience of the horrific experiences other survivors have faced. The trauma suffered by victims is unimaginable, and the victims are unsuspecting youth who find themselves taken advantage of because of their economic circumstances. It is her mission to provide long-term help to other survivors and to bring awareness to the mainstream how the girl next door can be affected by these awful phenomena. Vanessa will take every opportunity to show victims of sex trafficking that their story is not limited to that experience and that personal transformation is possible!

www.vanessajass.com

Baby Honey

Making Honey

I have the most glorious secret. It's a secret so beautiful that the thought of it brings an instant watery haze to my eyes, a toothy grin, and a catch in my voice. A secret so special, I wish I had a tiny, silver treasure box lined in Tiffany-blue silk to keep it safe. I think of this treasure thousands of times a day. I cannot imagine how people keep secrets like this one. It feels like you can see it on my face, as if I were the one *glowing*.

I raised radically cool children. I struggled. I cried. I doubted, and I often could not see the light. Despite my many failures and setbacks, I raised confident, intelligent, capable, caring human beings.

And one of these miracles, the oldest, is pregnant with my first grandchild. I am not allowed to tell anyone yet, but I am over the moon! I am going to be someone's grandmother. Me! My first grandbaby is in the oven! I saw the little cocktail shrimp in a photograph today, and as you can see, the love is already shining in this baby!

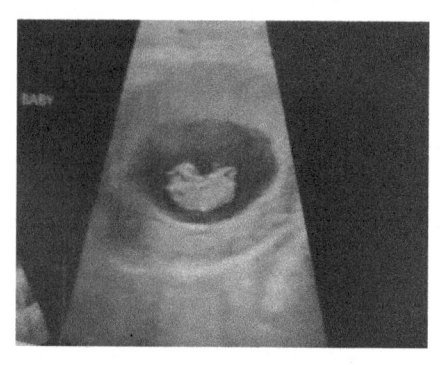

I am a long-haired hippy who sings in the garden, often with a joint, clothing optional. I howl at the moon if I feel like it and cleanse my crystals in her moonlight when she's full. I live on top of a mountain without electricity or water. I live in a manner most people would not even entertain as camping for the weekend, and I love it. I wash my clothes outside. I aim to grow the majority of my food. I bathe outside. I cook outside. I raise animals, lots and lots of animals. I have been living increasingly outside of society's norm over the past year. Prior to that, I was so codependent on my corporation and keeping my children alive and functioning that their beautiful ability to leave the nest and succeed on their own left me lost and struggling in a massive home with excessive staff.

When I finally, and I do mean *finally*, broke free from my own cruel imagination, limitations, and need to "keep up," when I could finally begin to focus on all that is light and wonderful in the world now that my kids were grown, I went wild! I could say yes and explore and experience things I could never have imagined back when I toiled in diapers, dinners, and date nights.

Did I say yes? I did! Or no, sometimes. The point is, *I said what I wanted and not what I thought I was supposed to say.*

I sold everything: home, company, building, furniture, trinkets, hoarded clothes. All sold or donated. I said no to anything that didn't bring me joy. I sold all the "things" I spent so much time caring for so I would have more time to play to my heart's content. Then, I spent a year in my RV, traveling the lakes in my state, getting to know myself. Guess what? I was not who I thought I was at all. I am so much cooler! At fifty-four, I am in the best shape and best mental space of my life and loving every second!

And now, I am going to be a grandma. My expectation is that this is a particularly significant role, and yet I am clueless.

I didn't have one—a grandmother "like that." The mix of the biological, step- and half-grandparents were merely temporary stops on Christmas day. My desire is to be an amazing, impactful, and wise grandmother, and yet I am not sure what that looks like. I know a lot about what it doesn't look like—so much so that only months before now, I was coming to terms with the fact that each of my children professed they would end our toxic generational curses by never having their own children.

The day my oldest told me the news of this tiny nugget, I drove the three-and-a-half-hour trip home in joyful tears. Then they were abducted by an old acquaintance of mine—doubt. My happy tears became tears of fear. What if I mess this up? I have worked a novel's worth on breaking heavy generational curses, and and I have created this incredible life that has allowed me to heal my body, my spirit, and my relationships with my children. My children have spent countless hours working on the effects of their dysfunctional start in life.

Grandparenting? I have not even started to study this. I know I am human, allowed to learn new things, and I love knowing this. I know what I want for this precious human life that I get to be a part of. I know how I want this child to feel when they know they are on their way to me. I can soothe my doubts in the knowledge that I have done the work. I have spent the time needed to make sure that on the day I behold this tiny face, I will be presenting the best possible version of myself. I love myself, and I know I will love this child like no other love. I love that they will have the coolest grandmother of all their friends. I am honored to accept this most humbling challenge. I am ready to be a grandmother.

I have already called the name, Honey! This chapter is dedicated to you, my tiny little honeybee. I simply cannot wait to meet you. With love and anticipation for your estimated day of arrival, December 9th, 2022.

Honey.

Honey is also an author in this book. She dedicates this chapter to everyone who has taken the time to do the work to heal!

Baby Honey • Making Honey

Honey is an international best selling author, a mother, a Woman and as it turns out, Ready! She openly expresses her vulnerabilities when she sees them and has found this to be an exponentially more joyful way to live. For the first time in her life, she knows she is ready for the next phase, the role of Beloved Grandmother, The Honey. Somewhere on or around December 9, 2022, Honey and the tiny Bee will begin their next and ongoing chapter together.

Hayley Vanderlois

I Am Stronger

We all think we know what we want when we're eighteen. Right? Wrong? I was not only wrong, but I also didn't know enough to know I was wrong. But like others, I learned.

Born in Oklahoma City to Donna and Nathan, I lived in Oklahoma until my brother died in a car accident in 2008. Two years later my parents divorced. In April that same year my father was killed in a car accident. When I turned sixteen, I was asked to leave my mother's house. I dropped out of high school in 2011 but earned my GED.

Let's call my first husband Connor. Connor worked nights and slept all day. I barely knew him and honestly didn't love him the way I should have. I didn't let this stop me from getting pregnant. Nine months later I gave birth to our beautiful baby girl, Kallie. We were already home from the hospital when we got the call letting us know our daughter had failed her hearing test. We had to take Kallie to a hearing specialist where we found out she was severely deaf and needed her first set of hearing aids.

Postpartum can be a real bitch, and boy, did I underestimate her power. Coupled with Conner being absent due to his work and Kallie's diagnosis, I fell into a deep depression and began drinking every single night. Then I had an affair.

Dalton wasn't my type and, honestly, he wasn't even attractive, but I was drunk and depressed. The affair ate me up so badly, I told Connor immediately. He sat with me, broken and defeated, but still asked me to make it work for our daughter. I chose Dalton and booze.

Connor took Kallie and moved two hours away. To go from being her sole caregiver to never seeing her broke me. I drowned myself further in alcohol. It wasn't until I was late for my period that I got a reality slap. I took a test and, sure enough, I was pregnant again. I told Dalton, thinking we would both be scared but that he'd be happy. He immediately told me to get an abortion. I refused. The first time he hit me was when we got in the car after our first ultrasound. Later, he apologized profusely and said it wouldn't happen again.

I stopped drinking because of the pregnancy, and it got really clear that I was in an abusive relationship. One night, when he was halfway into a bottle, I said the wrong thing. He hit me again. The first few times he said he was sorry, but after the ninth, I don't think he wanted to waste the air anymore.

What had I done? I was sober and alone in hell. I traded an absent spouse for an abusive monster. I dreaded bringing my baby home to this. To him. There were nights I'd wake up with him on top of me. Choking me. I didn't even know why. One night he got drunker than normal, if you can believe that, and the abuse quickly escalated into something more. He broke my phone so I couldn't call the police. Then he got on top of me and punched me. I pretended to pass out, but he grabbed my head and smashed it through the wall. I think that's when the neighbors called the police. I will never forget the feeling of relief I experienced when the police officers walked through that door. Dalton had passed out, and they had to yank him out of bed. He just sat there repeating over and over that he hadn't done anything. He is now in prison for domestic violence against a pregnant woman.

Jackson was born one month later, beautiful and completely healthy. Despite everything, he was perfect. I had great doctors who made sure that everything we did was in his best interest. I'll be forever grateful to my neighbors for calling the police. I will always wish I would have been strong enough to get out sooner. Recovering from a broken jaw, suffering from PTSD, and accepting my dependence on pills and alcohol for years, I was finally able to break free from addiction. I even learned a few things from surviving the abuse: one, I am stronger than I realize; and two, my kids are the most important part of my life. I look back on everything and I know it wasn't fair, but it made me stronger.

After giving birth to Jackson, I did the single mom thing until he was eight months old. Then I met Jonathan. After dating only two months, we got married and had our daughter, Avery.

Cannabis is what truly changed my life, not only mentally but physically and economically. I have been able to create a viable career in medical marijuana, starting as a budtender and now managing my own cannabis store. Every day I get the opportunity to change lives.

Hayley Vanderlois • I Am Stronger

Hayley Vanderlois was born and raised in the Oklahoma City area by her parents Donna and Nathan. She spends her time lovingly raising her babies and helping others find their path to joy and health through cannabis. Haley began working in the cannabis industry when State Question 788 passed in Oklahoma in 2018. She's run trim crews, cultivated and opened a dispensary, and worked her way from the bottom to managing her own store. Cannabis made such a positive difference in her own life that she decided to teach others the positive impact it could have on their lives. Nominated for "Budtender of the Year" in 2021, Hayley is widely known and trusted for her knowledge, advice, and skill in the cannabis industry.

www.facebook.com/hrussom

Elysia Stobbe

Revelation

Revelation is defined as an act of revealing or communicating divine truth; something that is revealed by God to humans.
– Merriam Webster dictionary

Have you ever been in an airplane when the oxygen masks drop out of the ceiling? No, I'm not talking about when you're on the runway and your plane is taxiing to get in line, ready for takeoff and the attendants are explaining to you what to do in the case of emergency. I'm talking about being on an airplane and the oxygen mask doors open and they actually drop out of the ceiling. The little square door above your head is released and pops open, and the mask falls down to your eye level. That's a terrifying situation.

Imagine you're in my shoes, sitting in my airplane seat in spring of 1993. All of a sudden the plane dropped tens of thousands of feet. There was no announcement from the captain. Everyone was silent; there was no screaming, no chaos, as the plane kept dropping. We were falling, falling. I looked at the other people in my row, saw fear in their eyes, and did what I had been trained to do from years of flying. I reached for that oxygen mask and put it over my mouth. With my fingers shaking, I put the strap on the back of my head, then over and around my head. While I sat there, shocked, my life flashed before my eyes. All of my brief twenty-two years were a blur: accomplishments, current goals, my good deeds, my bad deeds, the people I loved, all I still needed to do. I was terrified. I wasn't ready to die! It was so eerily silent. My stomach was in my throat from the sudden plunge we had just taken. I'd just accepted an amazing job at 98 ROCK in Baltimore, Maryland—a heritage AOR (Album Oriented Rock) format that has been in format since 1977, owned by the Hearst Companies. I was so excited to be offered an account executive position in one of the top fifteen radio markets in the country with one of the top five stations in that market.

I still had so much to give, so much life to live! Then, the captain came on. He said everything was fine. We all breathed a sigh of relief. They never really explained what caused our sudden plummet, but the question racing around my mind was, "Why am I here?"

That same question had slammed into me a year before. I was a recent college graduate with my bachelor's degree in marketing: business administration. I'd just left a successful job interview feeling proud in my new skirt suit. It was a beautiful muted green skirt with a matching blazer. I was wearing a white shirt with a pin on my blazer for added color, pantyhose, and high heels, trying to look as professional as I could for a twenty-one-year-old in the sweltering St. Petersburg, Florida, spring heat. "Why am I here?"

When I was fresh out of school, I had job offers in accounting and marketing that were not very exciting to me. On the day I first asked myself this question, I had been offered an entry-level position at a local radio station , owned by a National company, Entercom. I still had doubts about what I really wanted to do. I knew I was good with numbers and I enjoyed people. I didn't really think I was the corporate type. But if you've ever been in or around radio or the music industry, you know how much fun it can be. It's definitely not your normal J-O-B. Was it my favorite radio station? No. Was it a great starting point for me? Absolutely! It was a role I really wanted, and I was excited. The opportunity to be around music all the time, working with interesting and diverse personalities—this thrilled me! I had already done a couple of internships and was on cloud nine for being offered the opportunity!

I'd made plans to meet my roommates after the interview in South Tampa for happy hour. I was excited, as now this meetup had morphed into a celebration. My thoughts raced as I prepared my new announcement—all the excitement about what I would be able to do and all the things I would learn, the people I would get to meet in my new career, so many rushing thoughts whirling by, I couldn't even catch them. Perhaps this is what distracted me so I didn't see the stop sign and instead drove right through it. I had taken the back roads to avoid rush hour traffic, and I was probably going a little too fast in my little Mazda 323—maybe eight miles over the thirty mile per hour posted zone. I don't know how fast the other car was going. I only know it was a station wagon and that it T-boned me in the driver's side of my starter car, hitting so hard that my little 323 was knocked out of the intersection and up onto the lawn of one of the nearby homes, pretty close to landing on their front porch. My face was cut from the glass that sprayed from the windshield shattering on impact. The two front seats of my compact vehicle were now more compact than ever. The twelve-inch console gap between the front driver side and the front passenger seat no longer existed. The impact of the station wagon colliding directly into my driver's side door made it impossible for me to exit on that side. Realizing the door wouldn't open, I somehow calmly unfastened my seatbelt and crawled out the passenger side door in my nice new skirt suit. It wasn't long before I heard sirens.

The ambulance appeared, full of helpful, eager paramedics. They wanted to know who was in the demolished car. They were shocked when

I told them it was me. They couldn't believe I'd walked away from the car. I had crawled out of the car on my own. In shock, I had not realized this miracle. I hadn't been scared at all until they were all gawking at me. Within minutes they had me strapped down to one of those stabilizer boards and wearing a neck brace, concerned for unseen injuries. They whisked me away in the ambulance to the hospital. As I rode away, I was thinking, "Is this a sign? Am I not supposed to take the job at the radio station? Is there something else I'm supposed to do? It's my first job out of college. The first one I wanted, and I got it."

I'm not very religious. I believed in Spirit but hadn't really spent a whole lot of time in the church. My family was raised Presbyterian because my mother had renounced the Catholic church as she was raised. It's not like I had a true path to religion. Having always believed in God, I looked up at this moment and asked God, "Do you have a greater plan for me? If so, what is it? Please tell me."

Which is the very same thought I had on the airplane a year later after the captain came on and told us everything was fine. The can of worms was reopened. "Why am I here?" This time I was returning from another job interview in radio. My second job. Again, I interviewed successfully and was offered the position. Bigger market, bigger company and radio station—Hearst instead of Entercom. This would take me to the next level in a top fifteen market. I thought that's how you're supposed to do it: work your way up to bigger and better. Both times I remember looking up and thinking and wondering, "Dear Lord, what is your plan for me? Please reveal itself, please reveal itself. Thank you for saving me, thank you for sparing me. Please tell me your plan for me."

These experiences and the resulting questions took place in my early twenties. I didn't receive any answers, so I went about my business creating a great career in radio. Then one evening I was in New Jersey leaving a Tony Robbins Platinum Partnership event with my friend Kenneth. He had just gotten a new car and offered me a ride home to show it off. His new car was a beautiful, brand-new Maserati. I was having the most amazing time in my life, reaching all my goals personally and professionally, and to top it off, I was excited to see my friend. I wasn't worried at all when it started raining. I wasn't worried at all that we were speeding a little bit. Who doesn't want to flex their muscles in a fresh Maserati? It is easy to do…zipping through the busy traffic outside of Manhattan on the Jersey Turnpike.

Until there was too much water between our tire treads and the road. We began to spin and lost control quickly. I think we were probably going well over one hundred miles per hour. Yet again, time slowed to a standstill, even though simultaneously it all happened so quickly, I didn't know if it was me spinning or the car. Then another miracle occurred—not a single car hit us nor did we hit any of the many cars that surrounded us. Instead, we spun around three hundred and sixty degrees once, twice, three times, cutting across all lanes of traffic and then bouncing off the left Jersey wall of I-95 North, then across four lanes of traffic to the right Jersey wall.

The no longer pristine Maserati came to rest on the right side of the road. In a daze, I checked in with myself. I knew I was fine, I knew I had no injuries, and, remarkably, neither did Kenneth. I looked at him and looked at my own body that was in fine shape. The only proof of our hydroplaning spin was a tiny little blood blister on my left pinky finger. I had no idea how I got it. Everything happened so quickly. Maybe concussion, maybe whiplash, but no major injuries. Once again, I was fine.

I must have a legion of angels protecting me. I looked up to the sky and said, "Thank you, thank you for saving me. I'm ready. Reveal your plan, please." Still nothing. Nevertheless, I had been reminded that I do have a purpose.

I've been very fortunate. I have an amazing family, wonderful friends, multiple successful careers—first in radio and then again in the mortgage industry. I've been a best-selling author multiple times, and, still, I knew there was something missing. Something else I was supposed to be doing. People had told me, "You are the gift, it's your presence, you don't have to *do* anything." This is a beautiful compliment and very flattering. But I knew there was something more, and I needed validation.

Finally, on 2/22/2022 at a spiritual retreat in Tulum, Mexico, I found my answer. For those who don't know, 222hz is the love frequency. A small group of us meditated that day to send love around the planet, connecting with other aligned groups. The wonderful, peaceful joy in my heart grew, and in my mind's eye I envisioned a planet wrapped in love, feeling warm and happy. I pushed this image out from my heart center. I sent this beautiful feeling out to others in need of uplifting near and far. Through the long spiritual journey that evening, it was revealed to me in a vision that my purpose is to raise the frequency of the planet. Finally, validation had come! My gift is genuine connection and the ability to truly see others for their gifts without their shortcomings. By helping others see their own inner beauty and guiding them to their own truth, I help raise the frequency from doubt and fear to love, gratitude, and appreciation. My suggestion: it never hurts to ask, "Why am I here?"

Elysia Stobbe is the #1 Best-selling Author of the Pulitzer Prize–nominated book, *How to Get Approved for the Best Mortgage Without Sticking a Fork in Your Eye*™, as well as the #1 New Release *Journey to Success*. As one of the nation's leading mortgage experts with almost two decades of experience, Elysia has been featured in *The Wall Street Journal, U.S. News & World Report*, and on the Wall Street Business Radio Network, NPR, FOX, ABC, NBC, CBS, and others for her expertise with mortgages and finance. Elysia has presented her "Secrets of Success" and "Managing Yourself and Leading Others" at Harvard University. For more information and other books by Elysia, visit:

ElysiaStobbeInc.com
ElysiaStobbeBooks.com

If you would like your FREE "Journey to Success" Quick Planning Worksheet with your quick start video guide, click here:
KeyToSuccessInLife.com

To start your own "Journey to Success", grab the weekly video guide here:
WeeklySuccessHabits.com

Susie Cicchino

A Cup of Abundance

I love what I do. I mean, I really love what I do! I empower other women to be their best possible version and show them the possibility of being able to dream again, which empowers me to help even more women.

I have always been an entrepreneur. As a former restaurant owner, I found myself working sixty to eighty hours a week, yet I never had enough money and absolutely no time! I worked every night, every weekend, and every holiday. While others celebrated, I dreaded going to work. I spent hundreds of thousands of dollars to buy myself a J-O-B. Each month I struggled with less time, less money. It wore me out.

After constantly looking for a way to break free from the cycle of working for the next bill-collector call, I dove into personal development to empower myself. In 2006, I fell into network marketing after reluctantly and skeptically attending a sales demonstration. I never saw myself in sales, but as I got involved, I loved the personal development and the community it created. In 2015, newly divorced and reentering the workforce after sixteen years, I seemed certifiably unemployable; and *that* is when I cannon-balled into the pool of network marketing. Over the past twelve years, it has completely changed the trajectory of my financial blueprint, my impact, my family, my legacy, and my life, forever. The best part is I get to show my daughters what is possible for them too!

Thankfully, the person who invited me into this arena of life saw beyond my circumstance to find my potential. This is where I get to pay it forward, as a professional. It isn't about the money for me. Money is paper that is recycled. Money is impressive and great to have and needed to sustain life. It doesn't make life more fruitful. I now get to be a lifeline for those who need it in a way that I never have before. I found that the more women I empower, the more I am rewarded, which allows me to help more women. What a beautiful cycle!

I realized my true gifts: listening to women and empowering them. There are men in our business as well, and I enjoy collaborating with them; however, I have a unique ability to connect with and empower women.

My reason is simple: I never want another woman to feel like the old me, disempowered and desperate for an answer. I grew up in a family with old-school values. My dad was very strict and had a specific standard that I was expected to achieve. I should grow up, go to school, go to college, become a doctor, and marry a doctor. That was his plan. That was the persona he wanted for me. I had other plans from the start. I was the girl who always lived a little outside the box, who went against the grain and always wanted more for myself. I was the Big Thinker with grand ideas. I knew I wanted to be an entrepreneur, and I spent much of my time thinking of ways to own my business. While married, my ex-husband and I achieved this goal by opening a restaurant. He was a great cook, and it felt OK; however, it clearly was not a passion of mine. Then, the hours took their toll.

When I was exposed to network marketing, I first thought it was about having great products and sharing them with people. Very soon, I realized it was so much more for me. There was a community. We were building culture. Having grown up an only child, I now had a group of people whom I could count on. I had a family I'd created! And I could create my own schedule. Time freedom was a huge piece for me and allowed me to care for the well-being of my parents, to be there for them while still being consistently paid every week. I was able to be with my dad every day until he passed, and that time was priceless.

So now I offer coaching within the modalities I have learned and used to become the best version of myself. That is what I give back to other people. This ripple effect allows me to continue serving others. I get to see the light as it sparks and ignites within them. I build culture and community within my group of people. I empower them to envision possibilities beyond their current circumstance. Watching people transform is the gift I receive.

Through my own continual learning, I assist in removing limiting beliefs, move out of limitations, adjust mindset, define goals, and go for them! When I started, I couldn't afford to buy my products. Because of my limited finances, I was driven to find accountability partners to join me and get me started on my *own* franchise with little or no overhead.

My aha moment was realizing I could leverage my time and work collectively by being part of a community where we are all supporting one another. Many women have forgotten what dreaming looks like. For whatever reason, they put their dreams on the shelf and launch into a monotonous 40/40 routine, working forty hours a week for forty years—to get what? Life is short. Life is *now*! The past few years have shown us the importance of getting grounded and back to family life. Most of us have not had time at home with our loved ones for the past twenty years. The otherwise catastrophic pandemic allowed us to reevaluate values and find ways to live those values.

I work to create the abundance of overflow, not only to bless myself but to cause a ripple effect. To impact as many lives as humanly possible by sharing my abundance. This is similar to how money flows easier when we are following our passion, when we are fulfilled. At the end of the day, I put my head on the pillow and think, "This was a really amazing day. I mean a *really* amazing day!" It isn't my bank balance that keeps me in love with this life. It is knowing I make a difference. The fact that I am also financially safe and secure is the added blessing that came when I quit seeking financial wealth alone. When we have the skills, the mindset, and are able to snap out of a low-vibing state, we can accomplish anything.

Life will happen. We cannot avoid life or the dreadful things that happen. We can control how we react and how quickly we get out of that state. This is where the magic happens, by being able to push through those kicked-while-we-are-down moments without becoming a martyr or curling up in a ball. These responses are OK for a moment, for survival, but then we need to pick ourselves up and live our lives, whatever we can make of them, with zest and zeal and joy.

My coach, who is a lovely woman, explained that the way to give is to fill your cup first and then let people drink from your saucer, not from your cup. When your cup overflows, it blesses others but only once *your* cup is full enough to overflow. This is where we all grow and give! I work to keep my cup overflowing to bless myself and others.

Network marketing helps women work in the nooks and crannies of their day without taking away from their family or finances by offering them choices. They get to do what they love with people they love. They get to live their life aloud in a community of women that fosters growth and friendship. It offers sisterhood, a tribe where they comfortably fit in and grow into something much bigger. Some women get to reclaim an identity that may have gotten swept under a rug meeting others' needs. They find their worth again and realign with their passion. They get to be themselves again!

Once aligned, there is attraction! Thinking big and dreaming big allows us to surround ourselves with success that nurtures the community. If you hang out with five people who are broke, you will become the sixth. If you spend time with five powerful, uplifting, positive women who are dreaming bigger, you will become the sixth. With the right team, network marketing builds a community of people who lift each other up! Once we attach ourselves with those that are driven, and who think bigger and outside the box, we cannot help but be part of the collective transformation.

Which is why we need to be thoughtful, self-aware, and selective about who we invite into our lives, community, and network. Once upleveled, the people in our circle create a distinct, awesome bond of connected sisterhood. Welcome to absolute wealth. Be a light for others and assist in massive changes in lives. Let your cup overflow abundantly into a lasting legacy.

Susie Cicchino was born in Brooklyn, raised on Long Island, and migrated as a teenager to New Jersey where she has lived most of her adult life. She is a single mom who raised two beautiful, successful daughters, Sofia and Gaby, and her mission is to show them how to empower themselves as women and to live an abundant life. She is especially passionate about empowering other women, pouring belief into them, showing them how to dream again and live a life full of possibilities. She has built a community of like-minded women who help inspire each other and build each other up. Susie considers her spirituality, faith, and family to be most important to her. If she isn't spending time with Mike, friends, and family, you can almost always find her at the beach, which is her happy place. *Here Comes the Sun* is her first published writing.

www.facebook.com/sciccl
IG @susiecicc
@susiecicchino | Linktree

Shay Wood

Plan to Change

I have always been a girl with a plan. Whether it was a long-term plan or just having a plan for the day, I have always functioned better in a planned situation. In 2020, things did not go as planned.

I went to college with a plan to graduate with a geological engineering degree that would lead me to a career in the oil field. In 2016, I graduated from the University of Mississippi and moved to Houston to work as an engineer doing wastewater treatment design for refineries. After about six months, I started working as a fracturing engineer in the oil field. This was the plan! I had done it. I was working in the oil field. Two weeks on, one week off. I was in the middle of nowhere with a crew of guys, working the job I wanted to work, coveralls, hard hat, steel toe boots, and all. This is not a glamorous job, so if you asked most of my family and friends, they would tell you they were shocked that it was what I wanted to do. I did it not only because I got to be outside all the time but because I made a lot of money.

I had goals to grow in the company, which I quickly did, which was a bit shocking for a female in a "man's world." I went from an Engineer in Training in 2017 to a Lead Engineer in 2020. Three years is fast on anyone's timeline, plus I cross-trained to learn a completely different side of the business. I was a twenty-five-year-old female engineer in the oil field, working sixteen-hour days, two weeks on, one week off. Not only did I know the fracturing side of the business, but I learned the pump down perforating side of the business. These words won't mean much if you don't know the oil business, but let's just say I was the first in a company of one hundred thousand to learn and successfully run both sides of the operation on-site at the same time. It was hard, but I had a plan, and I did it.

I was dedicated to the company. I loved what I was doing and seriously planned to work for this company the rest of my career. I worked my ass off to hit that *last promotion*. The last promotion for the engineer track usually meant an office job. An office job meant no more sweating my butt off and no more freezing my butt off. Did I enjoy working outside? Of course. But there were times that it wasn't fun. This last promotion would mean I could finally get to stay at home with my husband and work a normal nine-to-five schedule. Although I really enjoyed this lifestyle, it was starting to weigh on me, and I was ready for that role in the oil industry that was a bit more "glamorous."

It was April 2020 when I got a call. The pandemic had hit, and the oil field was slowing down. I expected the call to be a job offer for a sales role, since I had my promotion. My husband and I had been talking about what our lives would look like with me getting to be home more often. We were excited. The call was not what I was expecting. It was a job offer, but it was for a fracturing engineer role in Midland, Texas. The same thing I had been doing for three years but farther away from home. What was I going to do? Leave my husband and keep working in the field for even longer? That was not what I wanted. After about a minute's discussion, my husband reassured me that I could take a layoff and we'd be fine. So I did.

2020 was rough. My busy lifestyle went from one hundred to zero quickly. I was not working; my husband was working from home. I had no idea what to do with myself. This was not my plan. My plan was to be a successful female in the oil industry and to bring home an income equal to my husband's. I am not the type of person who can just sit around and do nothing, so this was really challenging.

I could have gone into a deep depression. Literally, I felt like the world as I knew it had just shattered. As the days went by, my brain ran through the scenario where I stayed with the company and took the job in Midland, which was a good exercise because I realized I would have been unhappier being away from the person I loved the most, so I didn't get down on myself. Instead, I stayed positive and kept myself busy.

Then I stepped out of my comfort zone. I started a small spray tan business, which would be adequate until I found another job in oil and gas. Spray tanning kept me busy. It got me out of the house and allowed me to get my mind off the fact that I was not working in the oil industry as planned. Being a highly motivated and driven individual, I built up my spray tanning business quickly and secured many repeat clients. It was late July when I decided to stop looking for jobs and focus on my business until the pandemic was over.

August 2020, I got a random phone call from a man who worked for an insurance company, and he offered me a job. Insurance sounded boring to me. Why would I, an engineer, go work for an insurance company? It was weird, but I was talked into going for an interview.

After receiving more information at the interview, my mindset changed. In September 2020, I took a chance. I let go of what I had planned. I started working under an agent with the idea of owning my own agency. The company told me it would take a minimum of eighteen months to qualify for an agency. I liked insurance and was getting really freaking good at it. I quickly realized it was all meant to be. I was helping people—which is my passion—staying busy, and of course making money at the same time.

I took a chance, reminding myself it would be better to fail than to give up or not try. In March 2021, I received an opportunity to work under one of the most successful agents in Oklahoma. I took the risk and ran with it. I had a new goal and a new mindset. I had a new career and would own an agency within a year. That was the new plan.

When I said yes, I was blessed with the opportunity of a lifetime. I got to purchase an existing agency and take over as the agent. My original plan was to start a new agency, not to buy an agency, but I didn't let this change in plans stop me. I rolled with it. Not only did I reach my goal of getting an agency, but I also grew the agency, receiving recognition and awards in the process.

I worked hard. There were many days between my career changes when I wanted to quit or give up, but I am not a quitter. I would rather fail than quit. It's all about the mindset. I used to be the girl who was not open to change. I used to be the girl who wanted to stick to a plan. Although I have always been motivated, that motivation was to stick to the plan I had in place. A little change was fine, but most of the time, if I couldn't see something fitting into my plan, I wouldn't try.

I'm no longer the girl with a plan. I am happy my mindset shifted. I'm the girl who goes with the flow. I'm the girl who realizes not everything goes according to plan and that everything happens for a reason. I'm the girl who can step into an industry and climb to the top because I don't let things or people get in the way. I'm the girl who believes the best things happen when you least expect them. I'm the girl who takes chances and the girl who is proud to say I did it. Now the plan is to live my best life ever. And yes, I plan to change. You can too.

Shay Wood • Plan to Change

Shay Wood grew up in Henryetta, Oklahoma, in a family that always pushed her to follow her dreams. One of four children, she values the support her siblings provide. Shay attended the University of Mississippi, graduating with a bachelor's degree in Geological Engineering. In 2018, Shay moved to Oklahoma City, where she lives with her husband, best friend, and travel partner, Zach, her two Aussiedoodles, Paisley and Sunny, and her cat, Pip. Since shifting her career to insurance in 2020, Shay loves helping clients improve their situation by ensuring they are properly covered or by saving them money. In November 2022, Shay opened her own agency, Wood Insurance Agency, where she is happily helping new and existing clients with their insurance needs. The agency is growing quickly, and she looks forward to helping as many clients as possible.

www.woodagencyokc.com
@shaydwood
@woodinsuranceokc

Danielle Olbrantz

The Gift of Failure

I remember waking up in the hospital. It's a faded memory that almost feels like a dream, or a nightmare. A few days before, at one of the lowest moments of my life, I swallowed more than one hundred sleeping pills, hoping to end the miserable pain and overwhelming failure that my life had become. In the months before that day in May 2008, I had managed to create a mess out of my life. I had gone from an overachieving, successful mother of two who had my shit together to a complete mental breakdown. It was actually fairly impressive how fast I was able to destroy things, but, then again, I was an overachiever.

In August of 2007 I told my husband, who I'd been dating since I was fourteen, that I wanted a divorce. This was the beginning of me unraveling the picture-perfect life I had created. It was not an easy conversation. We had a three-year-old and an eight-month-old, and had been together for ten years. I had spent most of my teenage years and into my early twenties doing everything I thought I was supposed to: I married my high-school sweetheart; I started a great career in the mortgage industry; I bought my first house at nineteen; I planned both of my babies in a perfect two-and-a-half-year spacing; hell, I had even funded my 401(k). But in my million-dollar home with a view, I was miserable, and my marriage was emotionally abusive. My oldest child, my son, was one of the most difficult babies I have ever experienced. At the age of ten he was diagnosed with Asperger's and ADHD, which made being the "perfect mom" much harder, but that's a completely different story. I just knew at a deeper level that my picture-perfect life was pretend. Leaving my husband was one of the most challenging things I've ever had to do, but I knew that it was the first step in figuring out who I was.

The year after my husband moved out, I completely lost myself. I sold our home, which left me with a good amount of cash to live on—which was great, because the mortgage industry was starting to crash. I started by trying to figure out who I was and decided that since I had been "perfect" for way too long, I deserved to have fun. I ended up having too much fun. I partied any time the kids were with their dad, and I basically stopped caring about all of my responsibilities. This quickly spiraled out of control, which led to May 2008. Things had gotten so bad that my ex-husband was threatening to take the kids away from me. I had basically stopped working, burned through all my savings, cashed in my 401(k), destroyed my credit, and taken advantage of the few friends who were willing to try and help me.

It was bad. I didn't want to acknowledge how disgusting I was behaving, so I snapped. I couldn't live with the person I had become, and, in that moment, I really thought that the world would be better without me.

It has been fourteen years since that time, and I would venture to guess that 99 percent of the people who know me today would never guess that this was my story. I really haven't discussed it or told many people about that time in my life (until now, when I'm putting it in a book for the world to read). Today I am able to share that moment because I want others to see that things are rarely how they look. I want to give encouragement and hope and inspiration to someone who may be as lost as I was. I want to acknowledge the *gift of our failures*. I want to show that we are not our worst moments. I want life to be defined by how hard we work to rebuild, rather than how big our mistakes have been.

My real work began in the years after waking up in the hospital. I had to rebuild my life and, more importantly, discover who the real me was. I'd done a lot of damage. I lost custody of my children, had no place to live, my credit was trashed, my car was repossessed. I was in court-ordered treatment and had criminal charges pending. The mortgage industry was crashed, so I had no job. I had managed to mess up my tax returns, and the IRS claimed I owed them nearly one million dollars. I was not healthy. It would have been easy to just give up and accept that I would never live the life I knew in my heart I deserved.

I refused to believe I wasn't capable, and I refused to just sit and wait for life to work out. I started systematically trying to rebuild things. I had no real plan, so I just continued to do the next best thing, taking one small step at a time toward digging myself out of the incredible hole I had created. To say it was hard is an understatement. I moved myself and my kids in with my parents and focused everything on getting my life back on track. I completed eighteen months of intensive treatment, which satisfied the courts, so they forgave the charges I was facing. I went back to work doing just about any job I could get. With the entire mortgage industry in shambles, it wasn't like there was huge demand for the only career I was trained for. I found a job making ten dollars an hour, which was a far cry from the six-figure income I was previously used to, but it was enough to get by while living with my parents. Although I was highly overqualified to be a minimum-wage receptionist, I decided to be the best at it. I worked my ass off, and that led to a better offer, and better, and better. No matter what position I held, I was the best I could be at it. I continued to work my ass off for several years until I started to see progress.

I rented a house, bought a car, cleared my court cases, completed treatment, and got custody back. I fought like hell to get my son diagnosed and then did anything and everything I could to get him the ongoing treatment he needed to thrive. I slowly started fixing my credit, and I appealed to the IRS. After ten years of fighting them, I won my appeal and had my one-million-dollar tax debt reduced to twenty thousand, which I was able to pay in full.

I met an amazing man during those years of rebuilding, and his support was a big part of my ability to dig my way out. Paul came into my life exactly when I needed him. He had also been through a messy divorce and was starting his life over. Together we rebuilt. He was in the mortgage industry, too, and when we bought our first home together, we decided to take the leap to work together. (Truthfully, I was fired two days after we bought our home, so it was less a decision and more a necessity.) The path was never straight up and forward. We had many setbacks that we had to decide we would not let stop us from our dreams. We didn't always know what those dreams were; we just kept trying to climb to new levels, and when we got knocked down, we tried another path.

It took me until maybe two years ago to see the beauty in the failures. To recognize that those moments were not my worst moments but the moments that led me to discover what I was capable of overcoming. Previously, I'd been ashamed of those "mistakes," and while I recognize that I made some pretty poor decisions, how could I be ashamed that I was able to create the life I have today with the challenges I overcame? I was able to see that failure had made me a serious *badass*.

Tony Robbins has a saying: "Life happens for us, not to us." This sums up my years of discovering who I was and what I was capable of achieving. From the outside looking in, I appear to have a fairly accomplished life. I have everything I need or want and more. Paul and I successfully run a mortgage brokerage together. We have money in the bank, and our combined four children are thriving. My son, who I fought like hell for, is eighteen and going to school out of state. My daughter and I are especially close, and I am able to share with her the mistakes I made when she was little in hopes that she won't ever feel the pressure to be perfect like I did. But real success, in my opinion, isn't about money, cars, and houses (although those are nice perks). Real success is falling down and getting back up. Real success is messy. We often don't see others' messes because it's hidden behind closed doors. We don't see the tears and the struggles and the pushing through challenges. Some of us have to climb out of bigger holes to discover what we are capable of, but the ability to keep climbing and persevere really defines how successful we are.

Danielle Olbrantz • The Gift of Failure

Danielle Olbrantz lives in Northern California with her husband, Paul. They have four children in their blended Brady Bunch–style family. Danielle is President of Clear2Close, Inc., which is the mortgage processing company that supports Paul's mortgage brokerage, Clear2Close Brokers. They opened their companies in 2019 based on the belief that their customers deserved great rates without sacrificing personal and experienced service. In 2021 they were ranked the 49th Mortgage Broker in the United States by *Scotsman Guide*, and they pride themselves on always doing what is right for their clients. Danielle serves all of California and Nevada in their mortgage needs. The couple is also involved in a number of charitable organizations, and for the last five years they've rented a private movie theater each December, where they host children from a local group home for a Christmas movie, after which each child leaves with gifts collected from their annual toy drive.

www.myhomeloanteam.com
www.facebook.com/danielleolbrantz
www.facebook.com/myhomeloanteam.com
www.instagram.com/danielleolbrantz
Danielle@MyHomeLoanTeam.com

Laura Jennings

Free Your Unicorn

What stories are narrating your inner world? I wonder if yours sound anything like mine:

I am too much.

I am not enough.

I am failing at this life.

If I am the truest version of myself, I won't belong.

My body determines my worth.

I am the sum product of the things people think about me.

I need external validation to be OK on the inside.

These are just a few of the crappy stories that run rampant through the brilliant mess that is my mind. One of my friends describes this as her own private "parliament," as if these thoughts are like the men and women who sit around a table discussing the issues of the day. I feel like mine are more like the haggling guys from The Muppets who sit in the back of the theater and harass everyone with their commentary. Regardless of which analogy speaks to you, I am betting you have personal experience with what I am talking about, of being fully present for a moment and then the chatter begins. My mind is so *busy* and loves to tell me very detailed stories about what I just experienced. Some narratives are beneficial and even empowering and serve my greatest good; some are downright damaging. Becoming a witness to the stories I am *choosing* to tell, rather than letting the program or the parliament or the mind Muppets run the show, has radically transformed my inner life in the last decade.

Let's go back.

There was once a sparkly unicorn who shit rainbows and spread love and glitter everywhere she went. She loved herself, lived authentically, and didn't think much about what other people thought. A few painful life experiences led her to conclude that "her unicorn" would be safer all boxed up, where the shine and the glitter and the rainbows were not at risk of being rejected. The box was of her own making, constructed of all the limiting stories she told herself about who she was and needed to be. The unicorn believed she was a victim of people shoving her into that box, only to discover that she had imprisoned herself—one mental story at a time.

It was 1991, and Scarborough, Maine, was a place where winter felt never-ending, both seasonally and figuratively. I was a Third Culture Kid who had moved every two years since birth, from Dallas to Houston to Puyallup on the West Coast to Singapore overseas, eventually landing in the small town of Scarborough, Maine, about twenty minutes outside Portland.

On my first day of school, I remember being full of life. I was big and shiny and confident and smart and centered when I entered my first sixth-grade class at Scarborough Middle School. I was feeling *good* about me. I had become accustomed to being the new kid and navigating spaces that required me to muster up courage to vulnerably put myself out there or risk not having friends, people, or community. I stood up tall, found my desk, and sat down, my stomach filled with the nervous yet excited butterflies that swirl around one's tummy when a new experience is forthcoming. When the other kids sat down, I immediately reached out for handshakes like a middle school ambassador and boldly introduced myself, "Hello, my name is Laura Dauenhauer. I just moved here from Singapore." I learned immediately from how that introduction was received by the girls and boys around me that this was the wrong way to go about introducing oneself in this particular town where everyone was born at the same local hospital. The kids chuckled at my boldness and poked fun at my story, saying things like, "Where's *that*?" "Did you ride elephants to school?" As I tried to explain my real-life experience of living in Singapore, the truth of my difference from this group of kids became even more evident.

I took that experience, and I spun a powerful narrative that birthed an identity cord that became my tether for the next several decades. I anchored in the story that I didn't fit in and that there was something about *me* that needed to shift in order to create belonging. The story I told myself was that I was too much, too unique. I told myself it wasn't safe to show the fullest version of myself, and I decided to put my most authentic self in a box. I chose to dim my light to fit in. I became an expert at reading a room and determining exactly *who* I needed to be to fit in. It was too scary to be me, especially if I was a shiny, smart unicorn.

This was the pivotal moment where my egoic protector—that little voice of fear inside that has a single goal of surviving—loudly convinced me that becoming a shapeshifter would make life easier. Not belonging was too big a price to pay for my heart at the age of twelve; playing small felt safer. My time and energy became primarily focused on studying the "cool girls" and what hairstyles, clothing, language, gestures, and even eating habits I needed to develop in order to create belonging. I felt like Goldilocks trying to determine just the right amount of "muchness" to create acceptance.

As one can imagine, this didn't end up serving me long term. The more desperate I became to fit in, the more I sacrificed my authenticity and the more I suffered internally. I spent *years* of my life with this single story running the show: the box is safe and necessary because unicorns are too much for people. I took out that wide brush and I painted that story in bold letters across my mind and heart. And I had no conscious awareness that I did it. It's taken me thirty years to even awaken to the reality of the stories in my head, let alone unpack the power that I gave away every time I sacrificed my own inner belonging for external validation.

Here is what I know now: many of us are walking around telling ourselves a crappy story, mostly about ourselves. If our minds can run the crappy version, I will take a bold stand that our minds can learn to tell a more positive, empowering story. It requires each of us to make a choice to compassionately thank the stories for the ways they have helped us survive and then to release them and replace them with newer, upgraded versions. And we get to have grace with ourselves as we flex new muscle in each moment as we choose to step into a limitless story, full of freedom and possibility and inner guidance found only in present-moment awareness.

In any given moment, each of us is curating our own experience based on the story we tell ourselves, a story I find is crafted based on our perceptions, life experiences, and beliefs. Allow me to show you what I mean. My besties and I were standing in line at Elitch Gardens in Denver during our annual road trip extravaganza. Just standing in a random line, the four of us with a gaggle of kids at the same exact moment, each perceiving and experiencing a very different glimpse of the situation based on the unique stories being crafted in each mind. CM's story was all about making sure the people were fed and watered; all her achiever organizer brain could focus on was creating a plan to get fifteen water bottles filled up so no one would die of dehydration. LB was formulating a detailed exit strategy in the event there was a live shooter because her story was that we were all sitting ducks about to meet our untimely death. (What would we do in this life without our Enneagram 6s, for real!?) KT was in deep internal thought about how grateful she was that she was in a better mental spot this year because she was a complete shitshow at this very place one year ago. And I was in la-la land creating my own narrative about how each of the people around me were feeling and how much I loved them all. Same moment. Four extremely different experiences and stories, shaped by each person's personality, life experience, and, I dare say, neuroses. Y'all. This is happening inside each of us.

Every.

Single.

Second.

And there is power in the observation of it. It allows us to see and observe and take agency over our own minds and decide: who do I want to be in this life and what stories do I want running the show?

My life changed for the better when I powerfully paused, got still, and got real with myself about the stories that were running like well-paved goat trails. I awakened to the fact that I am an embodied soul who has a mind but is not run by my mind. I realized that I am the observer and witness of my thoughts; they do not just get to just run on autopilot, keeping me small for years and years.

So I have a question for you: when you get really still and quiet and connect with yourself, what stories do you hear? Are they kind, uplifting, and full of possibility? Or are they negative, nasty maniacs who tell you that you are unworthy, too much, or not enough? What I am here to share, encourage, and hug your little soul with is the truth that you have the power to *choose* which voices and stories you are going to listen to, trust, and believe. Because *you* are in there, and your soul is the boss of your own damn mind. The world is desperate for your particular shine, sparkle, and genius. You matter, your voice matters, and no one can shine in the way that you can with your unique tapestry of life experiences, gifts, and talents. Own a powerful story and shine your authentic Light. Our world needs more unicorns busted out of boxes.

Laura Jennings lives in Austin, Texas, with her husband and three children. She is a Third Culture Kid who attended high school at International School Bangkok and graduated summa cum laude from the University of Illinois and the University of Texas–Austin, obtaining her bachelor's and master's degrees in Communication Sciences and Disorders respectively. She works as a Medical Speech-Language Pathologist at Texas Neuro Rehab Center, helping patients restore their communication, cognition, and swallowing while recovering from traumatic brain injury.

She is passionate about helping humans discover the most free and authentic version of themselves through practices of breath work and somatic healing. She is known for her extra-long hugs, her solar-powered nature, and her deep affection for her epic community of badass women. You can find her:

www.instagram.com/sol.hug/
www.facebook.com/laura.d.jennings/about/
www.sol-hug.com

Brenda Long

Sunshine and Lollipops

As I reflect on my life from age six, I was an excited little girl ready to conquer the world and do everything that was good in life. And there was so much good in life. However, time and circumstances—some in my control, many not—changed the lens with which I viewed other people and my future. Just for a while.

My parents loved each other deeply for the twenty-five years they were together. With their "honeymoon" relationship, my four siblings and I had a front row seat to observe true love. They instilled in us a tremendous faith in God from an early age. It wasn't a perfect life, but they shielded each other and their family with love. I am grateful for this foundation; otherwise, the trials I encountered would surely have had a much more tainted lens.

The loss began with multiple deaths in one year. We had three immediate family members die within a thirty-day period: my grandmother, mother, and nephew. At age sixteen, I lost my father. This was the most difficult and distressing of all due to my age and the lack of security it caused me to feel.

Loss from death then combined with abuse, marriage, divorce, remarriage, and blended family, all of which positioned me to view life with a different but interesting lens. Life experiences created many emotions: happiness, sadness, anger, joyfulness, fear, insecurity, humor, judgement, thankfulness, trust and/or or lack of it, and pride. Pride is the one we all believe we have no part of.

For me, the most negative emotion that framed my life was disappointment. I built a "thinking muscle" and convinced myself I would always eventually be disappointed. It was a current of emotions that began in my head, with my thoughts. *As a man thinketh, so he is.* I overthought everything.

The insecurity I felt from my father's death created a powerful emptiness, and I had no boundaries or coping strategies to stop the ripple effects. As an adult, I threw myself into work and family, and, subconsciously, I believed I could handle it all. And I did for many years.

It is funny how the things I thought were so good for me were often a distraction from the best or most important things in my life. Strength is generally considered a healthy trait. For all intents and purposes, it is; however, even with strength there must be moderation. Our bodies are designed to handle the occasional stress in life, recover, and return to calm. We are not intended to run in a state of stress continuously. If we do not stop and allow our body to rest and refuel, we will eventually be running on nothing but fumes. As humans, we deserve to be better to ourselves than that.

Among the many lenses through which I viewed my circumstances, the most challenging was seeing myself as having the whole truth in each situation. It was my blind spot. Then I realized that no one can truly see their faults. This realization brought the beginning of freedom. It was as if being able to identify with others enabled me to trust and admit my shortcomings more easily. Choosing to truly look at myself in the mirror and see my faults allowed me to have more compassion and less judgment of others. *And* of myself.

These changes and awareness made the sun shine a little brighter; however, getting to this vantage point often takes a drastic event. Not always, but for me it did. I believe it depends on how well we build that "strong" muscle. It also depends on how tired we are of trying to control life, of clutching to make life work physically and mentally.

I was finally ready to embark on a new way of life. With my foundation in the Lord, fully believing and trusting Him, I set out to determine to learn more about myself and grow. My first role was to begin taking responsibility for myself, my intentions, and my life. Previously I drifted, trusting and believing that everything would work out, which caused me to roll with whatever came long, instead of setting an intention for what I wanted. I saw God's part as already done, as He continues to show His grace and mercy in my life. For what part others play, I accept that I have no control over other's actions. I can only control who I allow in my life and my reaction to those around me.

Before I could truly be all right with past events, I had to spend hours healing my hurts and owning how I'd hurt others. The healing required tremendous grace and compassion for myself and for others.

I needed healing from those unfair, unfortunate events, which required forgiveness so I could move forward without blame. Until I healed, I needed something or someone to blame to be able deal with the hurt. Blame holds others responsible instead of being responsible for one's self. I finally refused to give anyone else that kind of power over my life again. That is true freedom. I struggled to get to a place where there was no one else to blame, no one else to point a finger at for the problem. Taking responsibility for myself required that I stop blaming others, which wasn't easy, because it encompassed a lot of things that were not fair. I had to accept that even when I was wronged, I had the choice to forgive; otherwise, I would remain a victim. Period. This is true of all things, good/bad, right/wrong; otherwise, we will be pulled along by a current of excuses.

I want to be extremely sensitive to those who have had hurts I have not experienced, and therefore cannot understand, and for those not yet in a place to deal with the hurt. I was there. It takes time and the right kind of awareness, support, and courage. We must all walk our path at our own pace.

There were many years I tried to mentally change myself, or worse, tried to change others. I meant well, but it was a complete failure. I did not know who I was or what my purpose was. I always ended up in the same place, mostly frustrated. Finally, in facing the fact that I am the only person I can change and only by working on me, there was progress. Not perfection, but major progress.

I have to deal with the mental chatter that keeps discontentment and insecurity alive. I continually work on staying in complete awareness of what I am doing and thinking about. I surround myself with wonderful women who also want to grow and work intensely on who they are as individuals, loving unconditionally without judgement or complaint. These women allow me to share their lens so that I can observe situations, negative or positive, from a different perspective, and to then set intention, which is a choice. It is a daily choice, and it is worth it.

A lot of my actions and thoughts were habits. I have a favorite poem on my desk, believed to have been written by Lao Tzu, that describes the detriment of not living a life of intention.

Watch your thoughts, they become words,
watch your words, they become action,
watch your actions, they become habits,
watch your habits, they become character.

Doing life out of habit instead of intention can create a tremendous mess. This is where the large, round, multicolored lollipop in the title of this chapter has significance. I envision different colors to signify the changes in life—some dark, some light. It is sweet and yummy, yet sticky and messy. When I had one as a kid, it was something I wanted to share. It takes me back to a joyful place in my childhood when I think of one.

Looking back at the hard spots in my life, I firmly believe the Lord plans our steps, and He will use us to help others along the journey, if allowed. Every step taken (or not taken) brought me to where I am today, and I am OK with that.

If you are reading this book, it is my hope that you are OK with yourself, or if you aren't that you choose to find a way to be. I pray this chapter guides and gives you inspiration to choose to work on your best self.

I have taken responsibility for myself, set boundaries, and allowed others to be who they are (it is their life after all). I want to emphasize that this transformation is a continual process. It is not perfection. It is a blended, perpetual process of learning, healing, forgiving, and growing.

I cannot fully express the ease and grace I feel today. The tools mentors have given me to help in the challenging days are priceless. I am thankful for my husband who has always made life fun and has an amazingly positive attitude, even in challenging times. My heart is full of gratitude for my children and grandchildren, for their love and grace. I appreciate my family, mentors, circle of women, and friends who choose to love unconditionally and help me heal, grow, and learn.

It is my heart's desire to give others an opening to let the sun shine a little brighter in their life. To help others who are searching to heal and grow past the same hurts I have experienced in order to be all they were meant to be. And, mostly, to build awareness that while it is painful to heal, it brings great rewards.

Brenda Long • Sunshine and Lollipops

Brenda Long lives in Grapevine, Texas, with her husband of thirty-two years and their boxer, Max. They have four grown children and five grandchildren. Brenda has worked in insurance and finances for over 20 years. She was blessed to be in an environment that encouraged self-growth while working. A few years ago she started a journey of intentional growth to work specifically on herself. This afforded her wonderful mentors, tools, and sisters who surround her with unconditional love. She is grateful to have the opportunity to be a part of this journey.

Blong77@yahoo.com

Lily Quach-Dinh

My Sunshine Connection

This book is about the sun rising up, erasing shadows, and shining its light through each of us. Food is my sunshine connection. Cooking is how I shine my light.

My first memories of cooking were from a very long time ago when I was too short to see the pots and pans on the stove as my mom cooked. My dad built a standing bench for me so that I would be able to see better. That then became my standing bench to do dishes.

I vividly remember my first cooking lesson from Mom. She was making some type of canh, a Vietnamese word for *soup*, telling me how to measure in the fish sauce—half a ladle to start, based on how much liquid you have, then adding as needed to taste—along with some salt, black pepper, and MSG. When your soup is just about done, you add some chopped cilantro and/or green onions to top it off as garnish.

Then there is the rice. I love the simplicity of rice. It adds to whatever else is involved in the meal. I was taught how to cook rice on the stove. No rice cooker. To this day, I think that is the one important thing you must know how to make on a stove.

I don't recall cooking with my mom much after my first soup memory. I guess it was because I started school. I find it odd that I can't remember, but as I grew up and moved out on my own, having no one to cook for me, I started to cook for myself. A friend taught me how to cook

Bun Rieu, my favorite noodle soup. Bun Rieu is a savory crab and shrimp paste noodle soup with pork, tofu, and tomatoes. It is served with vermicelli and a side of fresh vegetables, including a toss of bean sprouts and thinly sliced green cabbage with a little bit of the red cabbage to give it an appealing look. Then it's topped off with mint, cilantro, basil, and some other seasonally available herbs. Oh! You can't forget the fermented fish paste and chili peppers to give it a kick. I like lots of vegetables and fruit and creating food with a spicy kick!

After I met my husband, Vu, and we started our life together, I ended up cooking every day, making various Vietnamese dishes to pack and take to work for our lunch. Then when the kids came along, I cooked even more with a variety of foods. I didn't want my kids to grow up being picky or unhealthy eaters, so I always included vegetables in our meals. Whether they were Vietnamese dishes or any other, there would always be vegetables. In fact, I really prefer all my meals with a variety of vegetables. When there aren't any vegetables, the food just doesn't seem right.

Growing up, one of my favorite vegetables was the bitter melon. My mom would cook it in different ways, from stir-frying it into eggs as an omelet or making different soups out of it. Due to its bitterness, not a lot of people like it, but I've been told by elders and seniors that as they get older they tough it out to eat it for such benefits as helping control diabetes or other health challenges.

My middle child is the only one who likes the bitter melon like I do. My husband, along with my oldest and youngest children, are not fans. However, they would eat it if I made it. My rule is, if it's in your bowl or on your plate, you are to eat it.

While cooking for my family, my husband, and kids may seem a daily requirement or chore, I enjoy doing so. However, I'd much rather be told what to cook than decide myself and then have to cook it. I don't like having to make that decision.

We are a family of five that enjoys our food. My husband and kids have a healthy appetite. I learned to cook other dishes that wouldn't be the normal everyday dishes served at home. I learned how to make pho, a beef noodle soup that my husband and kids love. However, there are some dishes I refuse to make or learn how to make because I don't eat them. This is unfortunate for my husband and kids. If they want to eat foods I do not make, they must either go without, find it at restaurants, or have other family members cook that dish.

Since I am not a fan of pho, I will also make a pot of Bun Bo Hue, a different type of beef noodle soup that is more savory and spicy. And at times there will also be a third pot, Bun Rieu (my favorite). These all take a lot of preparation time, and the broths require many ingredients, ranging from the herbs and spices to the final garnishes to top off before serving, but I enjoy making and serving them. Three different pots of soups is obviously way too much for a family of five, so I invite other family and friends over. I have had up to five other families over to eat, some having a bowl or two of each soup and even taking some to go. Seeing how much everyone is enjoying the food and company makes all that work worth it.

With my kids getting older, they tend to help when I ask. You see, I don't like other people in my kitchen, so they know to stay out of my way until I actually call on them for help. And if you are invited over, it's for a meal to enjoy, relax, and hang out, that is it. Guests don't wash the dishes or help clean up.

My favorite fruit is durian, a tropical fruit that is not liked by many due to its smell. People have said it smells like feet or something dead or worse! However, I think it smells great. I recall a time when I was peeling a durian and I started to eat it. My husband, not knowing I liked durian as much as I do, asked what I was doing. When I told him it was one of my favorite fruits, he looked at me and said he married the wrong person. For a moment I thought he was going to say he didn't like it, but instead he said he didn't realize he'd have to share when it came to the durian or even fight for it.

For someone born and raised in America, a lot of Asian people would think that I do not eat bitter melon or fermented fish paste, let alone cook with them. Both durian and fermented fish paste have a strong smell and taste. They are not an American thing. I know people who were born and raised in Vietnam and don't even eat those. So when I have gatherings, it's a good laugh when I offer up some durian.

Over the years, I would try to have a night where my nieces and nephews would come over so I can spend time with them and feed them, which also means giving my brother and his wife or my sister an evening when they wouldn't have to worry about dinner. As the kids got older and started school, those nights became scarce. So holidays and weekends were it.

Now, with my kids all grown up and out of the house, I try to do a weekly family dinner where we all sit and eat together. It is a way to see all my kids and sometimes my nieces and nephews. Gathering to share food and stories keeps us connected.

I don't cook just for family. I love introducing Vietnamese food to friends and coworkers. It's a way to teach about my culture, as we have a conversation about the food, tasting various dishes. Sitting down to a meal with people is an experience of learning, sharing, bonding, and love. I just enjoy cooking and seeing how my kids, nieces and nephews, and other family and friends react to and enjoy the food. It makes me happy, and I enjoy bringing others together and spending time with them.

As for those not in my close circle, sharing a meal is a way to connect and bond. At the office where I work, we had a complete change and overhaul of staff, and I was able to get to know each a little better by what they liked, didn't like, and could or could not eat. I also think it is a great thing to expand their pallets and sometimes push them past their comfort zone. Food can be both exciting and soothing, but we must not stuff ourselves. Too much of anything is too much. It is the quality of food, not the quantity, which nourishes us.

This little story about food is my way of inviting you to take time to enjoy the experience of a meal, sitting around eating, drinking, having a good time just sharing stories. My connections with food and cooking give me great satisfaction, and I believe others share in the satisfaction. It is a sensory experience, the smells and colors and flavors. The selection, preparation, and presentation of cultural foods and flavors add diversity and a great richness to life. It is my sunshine, and my light, my way of sharing. Discover what pleases you regarding food and cooking for others. It soothes the spirit.

Lily Quach-Dinh • My Sunshine Connection

Lily Quach-Dinh was born and raised in Oklahoma to two Vietnam immigrants who came to America in 1975. She has an older sister and two younger brothers. She graduated from Northeast High School in 1996. Her first job was in the summer before her senior year in high school at an independent insurance agency as a file clerk; seven years later, she opened her own insurance agency and had a good run for about eight years before she decided to step back a bit and work for another agent she admires and respects, until that business was sold to another aspiring young agent who rocks! She and her husband, Vu, have three kids: their son, Alan, and their daughters, Alyna and Alyssa, whom she is proud to have as her children. Lily also translates for individual clients and a translation agency. She is grateful for her parents who taught her to speak and read Vietnamese.

www.facebook.com/LilyQuach-Dinh/about/

Mandy Cruz

Dreams in Motion

From the time I was a little girl, I was taught to think small. Dream small. Be seen and not heard. I lived exactly how I was taught until my twenties. How does a small-town girl who moved out into the world at age fourteen find the strength to make a difference in this huge world?

Well, let me start by saying, "Not easily." My childhood involved a lot of moving and spending time with family members in different states. Seems I was in survival mode from a young age. Learning to be invisible was on the top of my priority list: being invisible to men with bad intentions; being invisible to whoever I was living with so I wouldn't cause any issues.

By thirteen I had been moved so many times, attended so many schools, lost so many friends, that I knew once I planted roots somewhere, I would be there for a long time. Little did I know that within a year of those first wishes for stability, I would be uprooted again and moved to Oklahoma. Oklahoma is where I stayed. I bounced around a few places before finding a sweet apartment manager who allowed me to clean apartments for rent. I thought "Yes!" I finally caught that break!

I'd dropped out of high school in ninth grade to work and support myself, but I always wanted to graduate and knew, at age twenty-one, it was unacceptable to not get that paper. So at age twenty-two I went back to high school, worked as hard as possible, and graduated with a diploma by the end of the year!

See, you all, dreaming bigger made that happen. I was beginning to learn how to dream; but let me tell you, they were still small dreams.

Since I had moved so much growing up, planting roots and building long-lasting relationships was a dream that seemed unobtainable. I'd gone from being an invisible child to being a woman, still watching my life from the sidelines. I needed a home, and I wanted to own, not rent. In my mind that meant no one could make me leave.

House-hunting while making $8.75 an hour was interesting, but I planned and saved and made it happen. At age twenty-three I, bought a little three-bedroom in a cute neighborhood.

Then I started thinking about how lucky the people were who vacationed on the beach. I wanted to be lucky. By saving every extra penny I could, I was able to save enough money to take a vacation. Not just any vacation—it was *Jamaica*! I did it all while making $10 an hour. I did everything I could afford to do. This was a big deal for this little lady.

Next, I got on the fast track to living my life with purpose. I got my first promotion to management at my retail job, and I thought, "This is great! I'm making moves!" I'd gone from fast food to managing a large retail store. How does it get any better? Right?? I asked myself that same question until my thoughts grew bigger and then into a bigger dream. I wanted to be the boss. I wanted to do something meaningful to others *and* get paid doing it.

This is when I was asked to help someone with cleaning. I was paid and felt so fulfilled after they reached out repeatedly to say how much it helped them to have me there. There it was—my calling! I had finally found a way to live my purpose of helping others while being paid to do it! My calling, at that time, was cleaning. I was more than just a cleaning lady.

I was a part of every family and every holiday, every promotion. I was valued in their lives. I even had an author thank me in her book. That's big, right? My heart was full, but I wanted *more*.

All of the sudden, God tossed me a little miracle curveball. A daughter. Whoa, a daughter? A beautiful child who had all possibilities open to her, a girl I would never teach to think or dream small. I wanted Justice to dream *big*!

I wanted to make sure Justice had every opportunity to succeed. In elementary school, her teacher told me that she was extremely smart and I should consider applying to an advanced charter school. I was over the moon thinking my kido would have more opportunity than I did. We worked hard, and now she is headed toward something in the medical field. Mom score!

There was still more work to be done. Until now, the "lasting relationship" thing wasn't going quite as I planned, but I was still moving forward in life and knew big things were going to happen. I had an idea about how to achieve what I wanted, and I got to work! I was working every day as a single mother trying to get ahead, all while my heart wanted to find love and do big things. I stayed focused on work. I had big things to accomplish, and I was willing to work for them. Work, work, work. In the process, I forgot to take care of myself. I thought I could work and drink my way through each week. I'd gained weight, which piled extra stress on my body. My self-image was very low. I felt awful inside.

Let's not forget that daughter. The one who watched every move I made.

I decided to change. Change my body and mind. I got online and found a Booty Bootcamp. I thought "maybe I need a new booty," so I went every Saturday. I made some great friends, and we went to multiple bootcamps around the city until Groupon took us to CrossFit. I lifted weights. I was running, laughing, and sweating. I was hooked! I loved lifting weights. I loved pushing myself to my physical limits, then smiling while I kept pushing past those limits.

I decided I no longer accepted limits. I stepped out of my comfort zone and signed up for my first CrossFit competition. My team trained not just physically, but mentally. I was terrified, but I pushed forward. We completed the competition, happily ranking in the middle. Not first but dang sure not last. My body and my mind were strong, I lost weight, I gained strength. Having shown myself how it was done, I wanted to help others discover their potential.

Then, wouldn't you know it, in the process of rebuilding myself, I found the love I had always longed for. Chris is a beautiful, gentle, and amazingly strong husband. Chris knew my worth immediately.

He said, "My beautiful wife"—which I loved—"you can do big things in the fitness world." Say what? Me? I wasn't a professional. Well, that's where the next big dream began. I started classes and even paid for one. Two months of anxiety later, I started my professional certification process.

After cleaning three houses during the day, at night I buried my head in books to become a certified health and fitness coach. Yep, guys, there it was. I could now share my own story of success in weight loss and teach people how to become healthier humans. Cruz Crew Fitness was born. Now I live my *big* dream helping others do what I never dreamed could be done when I was thinking small. I coach others on how to use and treat their bodies to get the results they want. I get to live my absolute passion every single day. I get to help others make their dreams come true while living mine!

Now that's called living my Big Dream. Showing people how to become healthy and happy. Being a health coach has been so rewarding.

I've started taking nutrition courses to provide even more help to my clients. Through fitness I learned who I wanted to be and who I didn't want to be. I wanted to feel good and look good doing it, so I did it. I just did it!

It still takes a lot for me to say, "I am good at what I do," but let me add that I know how hard I've worked to be good at this life. Every day I tell myself at least once, "You did this."

The moral of my story is simple: We are not all given the same opportunities to accomplish our life's goals, but we can all use our inner beast to push harder until we break through what is holding us back. Don't be invisible, and don't dream small! Goals are just dreams you dared to put in motion.

Mandy Cruz • Dreams in Motion

Mandy Cruz is a forty-three-year-old woman who is stepping into her best self! She lives in the heart of Oklahoma City with her little family: one husband, two (almost grown) kids, and four furbabies. She owns two businesses, her cleaning business and her newest passion, Cruz Crew personal training and health coaching. She absolutely loves fitness and all things health related. Our bodies and minds are so fascinating!

www.instagram.com/Cruz_Crew_Training/

Martha Moon Gutierrez

Who Rescued Whom?

The path to suffering is the path out of suffering - the Buddha

Two weeks ago, I woke up from anesthesia. I couldn't remember where I was or what was happening until I felt an unbearable pain in my lower abdomen and it all came back. I had just undergone a hysterectomy. Doctors recently found a suspicious fibroma in my uterus and decided that *at my age* the best thing would be to remove it altogether. The pain was not only physical. All the emotions of a long effort to become a mother hit me like ice-cold water. Vulnerable from sedation, I suddenly felt old, alone, and a total failure at achieving one of my fondest dreams: having a family, the family I longed for since I lost mine at a young age.

I was born what they now call an empath. Back then people just called me "extremely sensitive." I always felt emotions very deeply, which was both a blessing and a curse. I was able to feel absolute bliss, joy, and love with music, art, dance, and beauty, nature and animals. But this also made me more aware of pain, injustice, and suffering in the world. Growing up in a big city, I remember sitting in the back seat of our car and asking my parents why there were children and old people walking barefoot amongst cars, asking for money, wanting to give them my shoes and crying at night thinking about them not having a warm place to sleep.

The arrival of puberty with its gift of hormone bombs made it all harder. I questioned authority, was in constant conflict with my mom (a lovely woman with a very strong personality that clashed with mine as we were absolute opposites), felt oppressed in a religious school, and was devasted about world inequality.

My dad was my refuge. He was a tall, strong, sensitive, and funny man. My boyfriends were afraid of him because he was really big, but his heart was even bigger. I fondly remember one cold morning waking up and hearing him say, "Hold on, little one, hold on, you can make it!" When I looked out the window, he had jumped into the cold pool to save a drowning bee. He always knew how to comfort me. Whenever I'd cry in my room because I was grounded by mom or facing a broken heart, he would sit silently next to me. And just hug me. That hug made everything OK.

My dad died suddenly when I was fifteen. He had a mild cough, which turned out to be a lung virus that killed him in ten days.

"He didn't make it, but we have each other," my mom told me and my little sister after arriving home from the hospital with a sad face and asking us to sit on the couch with her. "You're the little man in the house from now on," she said, looking at me. So my dad, foundation, best friend, and favorite person in the world was gone, and not only was I not able to feel my pain but now I was supposed to be the strong one. I didn't cry. My mind wouldn't allow it. I was expected to keep us afloat.

I was shattered. My tall, strong father was brought down by a little virus. How could I ever rely on anything again? It seemed even God abandoned me when the priest at the funeral said, with good intention but terrible delivery, "He was called to heaven because he was such a good soul that God wanted him by his side." Didn't God care that I needed him too?

Not surprisingly, the sadness and shock that should have come out of my body that day stayed buried inside. Like a ticking bomb, grief became anger and isolation, making me feel alone and unable to fit in. At sixteen, when the repressed emotions got unbearable, I swallowed a bottle of pills, hoping to free myself from the enduring hopelessness of my life.

After escaping the hospital to avoid being locked up in a psychiatric ward, I resentfully started therapy. I'll never forget that first visit, when the kind-looking thin, tall man said to me, "You don't like women very much, right?"

"Why do you say that?" I replied with the typical rolling-eyes-fart-smelling-wtf face of an emotionally constipated teenager.

"Well, you just tried to kill one."

He was right. I hated my fat, curvy, and inadequate body. I hated my mother. I was uncomfortable hanging out with other girls because I didn't fit in their world of shopping, boys, and partying. I didn't know then that this therapy would be the beginning of a long spiritual path. That kind man taught me how to meditate, and for the first time in a long time, I was able to find peace in the presence of my dark, raw emotions.

This spiritual path became my refuge. I dove into Tibetan Buddhism, became a yoga teacher, studied and taught Sanskrit and Indian sacred scriptures, mastered in Reiki, found an Indian teacher who shared the lineage of Tantra Kaula for trauma healing, and then I got interested in proving the benefits of spiritual practices from a more scientific approach. I studied neuroscience and biodecodification, creating a methodology of Neuro-Yoga. My search to relieve my own suffering became a dedication to help others get over theirs. I was able to heal myself by being of service to others.

I realized that my dad's death was the biggest gift he ever gave me. It opened the door to the path of growth that became my purpose and allowed me to help many people. I was blessed with being able to successfully aid suicidal teenagers (having been one myself), support terminal cancer patients (who surprisingly healed in the process), and people struggling with eating disorders, depression, anxiety, and physical and emotional pain. *My own hardships turned from tragedies to gifts.* I was teaching around the world at international yoga events, conferences, and workshops, plus I had a full practice and was making a living out of something I really enjoyed.

Still, something was missing. I had a very absent partner and was longing for a family. The pursuit of pregnancy was long, emotionally exhausting, and very frustrating. Every time I got my period or had another early miscarriage, I felt devastated.

I decided to move to the countryside and adopt a dog. I found a shelter where they had a Rhodesian Ridgeback, a breed I'd always liked and would help me feel safe in the country. When I got to the shelter, a car was driving away with *my* Rhodesian.

"Am I really that unlucky?" I asked? "Is the universe not willing to give me anything?"

The shelter staff tried to convince me to adopt another dog: a female four-year-old, mixed-breed rescue that looked like any other stray in Mexico. I wasn't convinced. She didn't jump on me when we met. We were both reluctant. I said I'd think about it, mostly to get away from being uncomfortable saying no.

Surprisingly, I couldn't stop thinking about her. I decided, with little faith, to give her a try. How could I know she was the one who would rescue me? She showed me the true meaning of unconditional love, the magic of forgiveness and living in the present moment. This sweet little mutt nobody wanted to adopt turned out to be an exceptional therapy dog for the kids with autism I was treating. She literally saved my life more than once, from chasing a mountain lion and scaring away a stampeding horse, to learning how to detect a rise in my cortisol levels when an accident left me with PTSD. She became my friend, my kid, my partner in crime, my family, and I was happy with her in my paradise on the mountains of Colorado.

Then I started rescuing one or two stray dogs every time I traveled to Mexico. Every animal I saw on the streets seemed to show me they, too, could be amazing like Leia, that they only needed a home so they could fill the lives of their humans with love.

In 2017 the Great Spirit had other plans for me. I rescued a pack of five dogs from the highway while traveling in Mexico. One was about to give birth. I took her with me to where I was staying, just until the puppies were old enough to find them good homes. Weeks later, Mexico had one of the worst earthquakes in its history. Hundreds of buildings collapsed, and thousands of pets and strays were wandering around, lost and wounded on the streets amongst the debris. I put together a *temporary emergency animal rescue brigade*. I also didn't return to my beloved Colorado mountain.

Three years and about six hundred rescues later, I founded Adoptalove as a legal civil association with the mission of rescuing, rehabilitating, and finding loving homes for strays. It became my full-time "job," except I was actually paying for it as donations ceased and abandonments increased with the pandemic. I used all my savings and sold my house to support the costly treatments and boarding for a growing number of strays.

Exposed to the cruelest acts of abuse and neglect I had ever seen in my life, I lived with the painful awareness that over twenty-five million stray, hungry, and sick dogs lived in Mexico City alone. Faced with sickness, death, and constant financial and emotional distress, I was surprisingly happier than I had been since I could remember.

"What is happening? Am I going crazy?" It was worth asking. The answer: I wasn't crazy. I was experiencing the bliss of purpose, mission, and serving others. I'd learned about unconditional love from my sweet dog Leia. I was inspired by the resilience of the animals I was rescuing, whose difficult past did not limit their ability to feel gratitude and fully enjoy the present moment. I was enjoying myself for the first time in my life. Focusing on serving animals kept me from overthinking my own problems. Spending time with them showed me how to be fully present.

These little strays taught me more about life, forgiveness, love, authenticity, and strength than any of my spiritual teachers in my thirty-year spiritual journey. The *burning desire* to help them absolutely transformed me from someone who struggled making decisions—anything from what to wear, choosing where to sit at a restaurant, or knowing what I really want in life—to someone capable of responding assertively to emergencies and making urgent life-or-death decisions. I went from someone with constant self-doubt and fear of failure to someone who put all her time and money into what her heart was telling her, despite it being irrational, constantly criticized, and riddled with setbacks.

I understood the Buddhist noble truths about transforming suffering. That burning desire came from the unbearable pain I feel every time I see animal abuse or suffering. I often get comments like "I would never be able to do what you are doing. I can't bear seeing or hearing about animals suffering. I couldn't deal with it."

Well, I found the trick: I can deal with what I see in the world because *I am doing something about it*. The stories and images still hurt my heart, but they don't crush my soul anymore. I know I cannot save them all, but knowing I am making a difference for even one life transmutes pain into blessings. I've learned suffering does not come from the situation itself, but from the feelings of powerlessness it evokes. As an empath, that can be unbearable.

Life will always present painful situations. When you choose to face that which causes you the most pain, instead of repressing or avoiding it, your exposure to the source of pain becomes an entryway into forgiveness, passion, love, and resourcefulness.

When we spend our lives running away from discomfort, distracting ourselves to avoid seeing what hurts us, we get lost on the way. We lose power. We lose connection. We lose the opportunity to face and feel our emotions and grow from them.

Two days after surgery, I came home, welcomed by my three adopted dogs. They didn't leave my side all day, taking turns kissing me. After a while, I noticed my deep feeling of failure at being a mom was gone. It had been transformed into a life-altering awareness.

Motherhood is not about breeding children. It is about nurturing others and loving them so much you are willing to give them your all, then one day seeing them go, feeling fulfilled knowing they are happy without you. That is a capacity women have, regardless of whether or not we have given birth. I felt at peace realizing I have seven kids at home, and I am a mother of over seven hundred little ones I have rescued, rehabilitated, and rehomed.

That maternal energy in me is creating Dog Heart Foundation to continue *saving animals that save humans* as emotional support and therapy dogs for people who can't otherwise afford them. I believe I can help other people heal their suffering by letting animals rescue them, just like sweet Leia rescued me.

Martha Moon Gutierrez • Who Rescued Whom?

Martha Moon Gutierrez was born in Mexico and has lived in many countries. She holds a master's degree in social sciences and is working on a master's in animal assisted therapy. Producing a documentary for human rights and environmental movements, and her own passion to relieve suffering, started her on a spiritual path to heal herself and others. A musician, holistic therapist, and certified Jivamukti and Hatha Kaula yoga instructor, she developed a method of Neuro-Yoga in which she combines Dzogchen Buddhism and therapeutic yoga. This methodology holds the lineage of Kaula Tantra, a method to relieve emotional suffering, and utilizes neuroscience, psychiatric nutrition, and biodecodification. In 2017, her spiritual practice shifted to the rescue, rehabilitation, and rehoming of stray and abused animals from Mexico. Her current focus is on Dog Heart Foundation, her new project that combines her love to help both animals and humans by training rescued emotional support and therapy dogs for people who need them but can't afford them.

moonmarty@me.com
www.facebook.com/marthamoonneuroyoga
www.dogheartfoundation.org
www.facebook.com/adoptalovemx/
www.instagram.com/adopta.love/

Ryan Williams

Dancing On My Own

Heart pounding in my chest, blood pulsing in my ears, sweat budding on my palms. A pit in my stomach that feels like a black hole sucking me inside a never-ending void that leads to the frightening unknown. My skin tingles in the least pleasurable way. My hair stands on end. The flood of a fresh, hot serving of self-doubt and self-deprecating thoughts fills my already buzzing mind: *Who are you looking at? Why are you looking at me? Why did they make that face at me? That person must think I'm ugly. They are judging my new clothes. They think I'm fat. I can't even go out in public without offending someone with my simple presence. I don't want to leave the house again. They don't love me. I am not worthy. Why am I so ugly? I don't want the world to see me. I feel myself getting bad again. I feel myself slipping into the suffocating suit of anxiety, and I can't stop it. I'm not strong enough.*

Anxiety (n.) (1.) Apprehensive uneasiness or nervousness usually over an impending or anticipated ill: a state of being anxious. (2.) *Medical:* an abnormal and overwhelming sense of apprehension and fear often marked by physical signs (such as tension, sweating, and increased pulse rate), by doubt concerning the reality and nature of the threat, and by self-doubt about one's capacity to cope with it. (Merriam-webster.com, n.d.)

These definitions just scrape the surface of what anxiety means to some people in this life, myself included. For some, it's a fleeting episode that only affects them for a short period of time and leaves just as quickly as it came. For others, it can be the top influencer of the personality we develop and the sole decision maker for the choices we make on a daily basis. Anxiety also shows itself in so many more ways than just sweaty palms and a racing pulse. It can be:

- Angry, white-hot, explode-with-rage-hurtful words you regret later
- Running to the bathroom at a big event because the constant changing sounds and sights are too stimulating, and you need a reset
- Stopping for that extra-large cheeseburger and fries on your way home that will inevitably make your gut feel worse, but you know you have more work waiting for you as soon as you step across the threshold, and the thought of preparing food is almost painful
- Telling yourself it's "normal" to need two glasses of wine every day to unwind
- Checking out completely and feeling like you can barely think, let alone speak or be engaged in any conversation
- Withdrawing socially and feeling like a burden to the people you love

My journey of mental health and self-awareness started before I knew it had even begun. I remember having anxious thoughts and feelings as young as eight years old. Coincidentally—or perhaps not (most likely not)—this is also when my parents divorced and my role in the family went from eldest child to caregiver, overnight. I started to feel as if I were different, like an outsider trying to blend in with people who could spot my abnormalities from miles away. I was homeschooled through elementary school and then thrown abruptly into the brash life of the public school system as I headed into the sixth grade. I was truly excited to start public school, make friends, and have new experiences. I felt that going to a "normal" school would help me feel more normal too. This proved to be an incorrect idea; in fact, it pushed me even further from the feeling of normality I craved so badly in that phase of my life.

While simultaneously dealing with the full swing of anxiety and depressive episodes, I am also an incredibly expressive and eclectic individual when it comes to my sense of style and self-expression. You might ask, "Now, Ryan, you don't want people to look at you, but you also dress like you have a giant red arrow pointed at you that reads 'PLEASE LOOK AT ME!' How does that make any sense?"

It makes sense because *I am not anxiety*. I am an artistic, expressive, creative, bold, social creature who happens to also *have anxiety*. Thoughts are the cause of all suffering; and while pain and discomfort are unavoidable obstacles we must face, suffering is ultimately a choice. Anxiety is fundamentally an expression of two major emotions we all feel in this existence: *fear* and *pain*.

- Fear of the unknown or what may come to fruition
- The pain of memories we have lived in the past

Anxiety locks you into these feelings when they have no business being part of you in the present. You fear what you do not know, so instead of looking eagerly to every beautiful thing that also could happen (manifestation is a powerful thing), you play out every horrible thing that could happen. The pain of difficult, traumatic, and hurtful experiences you have lived lingers in your subconscious, still crippling you long after the wound has been made.

So how do you escape fear and pain? How do you break free from the daily pattern of anxiousness? For me, I realized I had to do three distinct things:

1. Separate myself from those thoughts

2. Analyze them from a place that was separate from where they started
3. Allow myself to process these feelings without judgment

I allowed my consciousness to process my thoughts as if they were an entirely separate entity. I started to recognize when an anxious thought was arising, and instead of allowing myself to be consumed by or believe it, I would separate it and allow myself the time and space to break it down, understand it, and release it.

Like watching a bird flying overhead, I see you,
I hear you, I see you leaving now.

For example, let's say I walk into a room of business partners I've never met, and I need to make a good impression. Well, my first thoughts would be, "Oh gosh, I hope I've made every 'right' decision for the entirety of my career leading up to this moment because, if not, then they will view me as a failure." Then I break it down. Why am I saying this to myself? I want to be perceived well so that I can advance within this company. Do they truly expect perfection? Is anyone in this room perfect? Walk into any room at any given time and you will not find anyone who is perfect.

All humans long for belonging and understanding. None of us are immune. When I began to take a step back from anxious thoughts and feelings and allow myself to not only feel and hear them but also to release them as inaccurate thoughts, it became easier and easier to understand that these anxious thoughts were simply fabrications created by the fear of the unknown and the pain of my past. I realized I was a prisoner to events that I could not change. I was being held down and immobilized by the fear of what I could not control. I was so chained by both the past and the future that I wasn't allowing myself to love the present. I was unable to be who I truly was or the person I had the potential to become because I was trapped in a cocoon of hurt I hadn't allowed myself to let go of. I actively made choices to keep that cocoon wrapped tightly around me because what if I *allowed myself to love myself*? What if I stopped letting what other people think of me take precedence over what I thought of myself?

The more I separated these anxious thoughts, the more I understood and forgave myself and others for the pain I have experienced throughout life. It became easier to embrace every moment of every day with absolute open arms and the eagerness of a child experiencing everything for the first time. Through this experience I also was more free to look at my fellow humans and realize I am not alone in these thoughts and feelings. There are more people living in this cocoon than those who allow themselves to fly freely in the present beauty of the moment.

When I decided it was time to leave that shell behind and embrace my true self, I wore the beautiful clothes I wanted to without worrying what others thought. I wore them with confidence. I performed in plays because I love the arts and the warmth of a spotlight. I wrote comedy and put on shows because laughter is one of the most beautiful human reflexes I've ever seen. I sang loudly for crowds (though not always well) because I become alive and electric when singing songs that bring me joy. I allow myself the freedom to enjoy the present without being trapped in my past or fearful of my future. Heart pounding, pulse racing in my ears, the music of the night vibrating through the air, a familiar tune sparks happiness in my heart and I run to the dance floor and dance on my own, free of the fear of what anyone thinks or how anyone views me because *I am not their thoughts*. I am free. I am love. I am soul. I am happiness. I am bold. I am unafraid. I am present. I am alive.

RYAN WILLIAMS • Dancing On My Own

Amanda Ryan Williams is her given name, but Ryan has gone by her middle name since she was born in 1992. She spent the first portion of her life moving all around Texas until her family settled in Oklahoma in the early 2000s. Since then, Ryan's spent most of her years working in various restaurants and, in her free time, pursing her passions for acting and comedy. She currently manages a popular Oklahoma-founded Mexican food chain and is a part of their training team. She has three lovely cats—Grunt, Penelope, and Artemis—and a wild German Shepard named Guca-Molly, or Molly for short, all of which are rescue animals because she's a sucker for an animal in need. Ryan is new to the writing world, but she looks forward to the various writing opportunities she foresees in her future. Until next time, "Keep on shining, my new friends."

Facebook: www.facebook.com/thegirlryan13
Instagram: www.instagram.com/thegirlryanokc
Snapchat: thegirlryanmeow
Email: Locoforqueso@gmail.com

Dorothy Stangle

Reflections on Suicide

It has been a struggle coming to terms with that day in my life when I returned home at the request of the sheriff. He asked that I return home as soon as possible. I asked him if he could explain, and all he told me was that it was not something he wanted to discuss on the phone. I would later find out he obtained my phone number by looking through my desk.

On the way home, I reviewed the time I'd spent since leaving the house that morning. I had an appointment with my best friend that day, and upon leaving the house, I noticed my husband's car in the driveway. At the time, I figured he probably met someone who picked him up. While driving home, panic set in. I immediately called his office and asked his secretary if I could speak to my husband.

She replied, "Oh, Dorothy, we are so worried. He hasn't shown up, and we were ready to call you to find out if he was OK. He is never late for work."

My heart began racing. Something was terribly wrong. When I turned onto my street, I noticed several sheriffs cars and a couple of police vans. I knew then it was something bad. The sheriff met me outside. I noticed my husband's briefcase on the porch and wondered why it was there. My dog was becoming agitated, and one of the policemen asked me to put her outside in the screened room while we chatted.

We all sat in the kitchen, and the questions began to come one after another. As I write, a tear comes to my eyes because it is still fresh in my mind. I think it will always be with me. It was March 25th, 2015, and I still remember how I felt. I was shaking inside. The sheriff was the first to ask me if my husband was involved in anything that may be criminal. The answer was no. Was he involved with anyone? The answer was no. Did he have financial problems? The answer was no. It continued, and at this point I was sure he may have been in an accident; at least I hoped that was it. The answer was always the same.

I said, "Everyone loved him." I wasn't prepared for what was coming. They asked if I had received a note or if I had spoken to him. The answer was no.

"Has something happened to my husband?" I asked.

"Your husband committed suicide. He went to a vacant lot and shot himself."

I could only stare, paralyzed. The word "suicide" didn't register. It seemed forever before I could say anything. "Suicide? He shot himself." I was numb.

A crisis counselor who was among the authorities asked if there was anything she could do for me, then left a handful of cards representing support groups suffering from the trauma I would be going through. She hugged me, and it was hard to let go.

As I reflect on my journey through suicide grief that started seven years ago when my husband died by his own hand, I'd like to share what I've learned in the hope that it will be helpful. While grief is hard, you do survive it, and there is a community of suicide loss survivors and professionals who will meet you on your grief journey. One of the things I know for sure: whether you are prepared for it or not, grief happens, and whether there is room in your life, it shows up in both predictable and unpredictable moments, in images and memories that simultaneously bring joy and pain. Reflecting on the relationship with the person who committed suicide causes the grief.

Even though grief from a suicide loss can sometimes feel overwhelming, it is important to do as much as you can to take care of yourself as you grieve. Professionals advise you to take care of our body's basic needs—make sure to drink enough water, eat nutritious food, get some gentle daily exercise, and sleep when you can. Does it help? Is it even possible to do these things? It's all well and good, but it isn't easy when you are left alone with no one around to lean on. Consider asking a good friend or family member for help. Certainly being alone in a different state from where your family lives can be trying. You can't rush the grieving. It takes as long as you need.

My husband and I had been together for thirty-six years. Relationships are complex, and our experiences of their suicide are a reflection of that individual and the relationship you had. You can't know everything that contributed to your loved one's death or how you will survive without them. Be open to what you discover about yourself and what your relationship was as time passes. You will think differently about the loss as time goes by. Sooner or later, the healing will happen…or at least begin.

Grieving will exhaust you. Finding different ways to recover will vary from drinking alcohol to overeating. Attending support groups, church, other gatherings where you can find social support is helpful. There will be days when the grief is particularly difficult. It will overpower you to the point where you feel as though you've run five miles. I believe being present with your grief and sharing it with a suicide support group or a therapist could be helpful.

Make time for rest, and treat yourself to time for recovery. One of my problems was that I tried to be too strong, and I realize now that I should have reached out for help.

Don't let grief be a burden. It is expected. And never apologize for showing emotions in response to losing your loved one. It's OK to say their name. It enables you to speak about the loved one and will give others around you permission to talk about them. Sharing stories and memories can be healing.

Death by suicide affects not only you but others who cared deeply about the person. The shock and grief that consume you after losing someone to suicide can feel crushing. No two people experience loss in the same way. You will experience shock, denial, sadness, anger, and, most of all, guilt. You will continue to tell yourself, "It was my fault," which is very common. Guilt comes from the mistaken belief that we should have or could have prevented the death from happening. And if there are unreconciled issues with the deceased or regret about stuff said or not said, that can feel heavy. You can never know all the reasons for another person's actions. It is human nature to blame oneself when experiencing a loss rather than accepting the truth that some things are out of our control. Feelings of hopelessness, frustration, bitterness, and self-pity are common when dealing with the loss of a loved one. Eventually, you learn to accept the loss and embrace both your happy and sad memories.

Anger can raise its ugly head and you will ask yourself, "How could they do this to me?" You won't want to feel anger toward the person you lost, and many mourn and feel a sense of abandonment. It is possible to both be angry with someone and still hold them dear in your heart. Sometimes anger is needed before you can accept the reality of the loss. Feelings such as abandonment and rejection can occur after a suicide, as well as positive feelings about the deceased. Sorting through all these diverse, contradictory feelings can make the healing process more challenging.

Experiencing a loss by suicide can sometimes increase the risk of having suicidal thoughts yourself. These thoughts do not mean you will act on them. Thoughts like this will decrease over time, but if they continue to get worse, it is good to consider therapy. You may not feel like getting out of bed and dressing for the day, as this will seem challenging, so reestablish a routine as soon as you can.

Many people have trouble discussing suicide and might not reach out to you, leaving you to feel isolated or abandoned if the support you expected to receive just isn't there. Do what is right for you, not necessarily for someone else.

There is no right way to grieve. To this day, I find it too painful to visit my loved one's gravesite or share the details of the death. I suggest waiting until you're ready. You will know. Since losing my husband, I've experienced physical problems, and I did seek therapy. I remember wondering how I would get through it. I understand the complicated legacy of suicide and have learned to cope as I heal. I continue to honor the memory of my husband but have also learned that life goes on. Never give up hope.

Dorothy M. Stangle is an author and retired businesswoman, born in Hunstanton, Norfolk, England. Dorothy will be publishing her first book in 2023. A novel loosely written about her mother, who was born and raised in London, England, it is the story of a woman's struggle to overcome adversity as well as tragedy, always maintaining her integrity and showing strength—traits which she passed onto her daughter. Dorothy grew up traveling the world as an Air Force brat. Her father spent most of his life in the military, serving in three different wars. She is grateful for the strength she learned from her mother. It was much needed during a very tragic time in her life. She is dedicated to all those struggling to understand the complicated legacy of suicide and learning to cope with the aftermath.

dorothy.stangle@yahoo.com

Andrea Marie Yoder

Craving

When you're an ambitious person, all you ever focus on is moving forward. You are always seeking the next best way to better yourself. Throughout my story, I had many ambitions, but my goal was always the same: I wanted to live a life that had a positive impact on others. I'm sure most people reading this book feel the same way. I am a human being who has achieved many great goals in my life. Well, I think they're great. I am well educated. I am physically strong. I have a career that many would consider to be "elite." I'm a huge influence on a little blonde person who calls me mom. These are all great things.

This story isn't meant to discuss my strengths, though. This is a story about my having to recognize my biggest weakness, my craving, and learning to overcome it.

Unlike many of the warriors in this book, I didn't suffer any trauma or abuse growing up that made me drink. I grew up in a country home with a family filled with lots of dysfunction but even more love. There isn't a single human being in my family who hasn't suffered from some form of addiction. I am no exception.

When I started drinking in college, I envisioned what my life would look like in the future. I thought of the level of education I would obtain, what career I would establish, who my husband would be, etc. I never had a second thought that I was sending myself down a path from which I would later have to work so hard to find my way back.

Initially, I set out to be a lawyer. Not just a lawyer, though. I wanted to be the greatest criminal attorney the state of South Dakota had ever seen. I received a bachelor's degree in Criminal Justice with an emphasis in Pre-Law. I studied for the LSAT and was accepted into the law school I had been planning on attending for more than a decade. With the acceptance letter in my hand, I told my dad that I didn't want to go. What was the reason? I don't know. My gut instinct told me not to, so I didn't.

The next tenacious goal was to serve my country. I enlisted in the Navy with every intention of becoming a great officer. Much to my surprise, during boot camp it was brought to light that I had seen a counselor some five years earlier. To this day, I don't know exactly what that counselor wrote about me, but it was enough to have "ENTRY LEVEL MEDICAL DISCHARGE" stamped on my DD-214, and my ass was sent back home with my tail tucked firmly between my legs.

OK, so two unsuccessful dreams I'd strived for had fallen through. For the first time in my life, I had no idea what to do with myself. What did I do to pass my time? I partied even harder than before. My goal to make something of myself, though, was still very much in the forefront of my mind. I decided that I wasn't going to accomplish much of anything in a small town in South Dakota. Incrementally, I emptied my closet into the back of my 1999 Oldsmobile Intrigue and drove south. I stopped in Oklahoma City, which was the only place I had any other family. My aunt graciously allowed me to live with her rent free while I was on my quest to do something with my life.

A colleague of my dad's recommended that I become a firefighter for the Oklahoma City Fire Department because they were known for being one of the best departments in the nation. Mind you, I didn't know the first thing about being a firefighter. I figured it had to be an active job, and the title sounded cool, so why not? Little did I know, I was about to be accepted into the greatest profession in the world.

I can't say for sure, but I believe this is the place where my drinking became a "problem." The hiring process for the fire department took eleven slow months.

To make money, I worked as a waitress and bartender, just as I had done all through college. When you work in the service industry, you tend to work when everyone else is playing. The friends I made were the ones I worked with, and our favorite pastime was always drinking. My aunt, whom I had moved in with, struggled with alcoholism herself, which didn't help my situation. Let me specify that, at that time, when I drank, I drank strictly to have a good time. I never drank to "escape" or "drown" any feelings. I had a great life that I loved. This was especially applicable when I was hired on at the fire department. Look at me go! I had an amazing career that I had been trying to attain for so long. I had tons of friends and no responsibilities—two very good reasons to drink like a fish every chance I got.

As time went on, I achieved every goal I ever envisioned for myself. I became a paramedic. I met a wonderful man who became my husband. I had a beautiful baby boy. I was promoted to the entry-level officer's position on the fire department. I did it all while drinking. I drank to relax after a huge exam. I drank because it was hard to fall asleep after a difficult shift. I drank because it was a holiday. I drank because an eyelash was out of place and a beer sounded good while I reapplied my mascara. I even drank when I was seven months pregnant. I don't know exactly when the tipping point was that I went from "fun party girl" to "alcoholic suburban mom," but it happened.

My husband is one of the best human beings I have ever known. He was the first one to ever tell me that I was an alcoholic. It was in that moment that I realized I had reached many lifetime milestones and was still drinking despite it not being conducive to the lifestyle I was leading anymore. The fun activity that seemed harmless earlier in my life was now a spiraling addiction. *Instead of drinking because I loved my life, I had to drink to love my life.* This was eight years after I had left South Dakota. That meant I had been drinking steady for almost thirteen years.

My first pregnancy was what I called my first attempt to get sober, but it wasn't that. I had gotten pregnant by surprise. I was happy to be having a baby, but I didn't want to give up drinking to do it. The day I knew I was an alcoholic was the day that I realized I wasn't resisting drinking for the sake of my baby; I was only doing it because I didn't want my baby to have fetal alcohol syndrome, because I didn't think I could take care of a special needs child. It sounds horrendously selfish, doesn't it?

Even that realization wasn't enough to make me quit entirely. That same gut instinct that told me not to go to law school was talking to me louder than ever, telling me to quit, but I still couldn't at that time. During one of my *many* attempts to get sober, I saw an alcohol counselor who told me it took twelve to eighteen months to undo the chemical degradation that chronic alcohol use causes to the brain. When I heard that time frame, I didn't actually think I would make it that far. I thought I wouldn't need to. Like many people, I thought I could take a quick break from the booze and then come back to moderate it. Aren't I cute? The more I tried to moderate, the more booze I wanted.

In spite of how far I had already spiraled, the ambitious girl who left South Dakota over a decade earlier was still buried deep in my little booze-filled brain. That girl didn't like to admit that she had a weakness. My sober date was the day I admitted to myself that I had a massive weakness for booze that began in college and had gradually built up over time. The cravings were unimaginably strong at first, but they have weakened over time. As every person in recovery does, I battle that weakness daily for the sake of this: *living a life that has a positive impact on others.*

If nothing else is taken from my story, I would love anyone reading this to understand that alcoholism takes many forms. It looks different on everyone. It doesn't just happen to the emotionally traumatized or downtrodden. As difficult as it can be for a girl to admit she has a weakness, sometimes that admission is the only thing standing in the way of the proudest accomplishment in her life. I know it was for me.

Andrea Marie Yoder • Craving

Though her social security card reads Andrea Marie Yoder, she's only called that when she's in trouble. Her name is Andi. She's a simple country girl who grew up just outside of Rapid City, South Dakota, where she lived until she was twenty-three. She grew up working her family's land alongside her dad and the rest of her family because they couldn't afford to hire help. She currently resides in Yukon, Oklahoma, with her incredible husband and their two-year-old whirling dervish, Maximus. Andi is a paramedic firefighter for the Oklahoma City Fire Department. She has the greatest job and works for the greatest department in the nation. To whomever reads her story, her hope is that it finds you in a state of grace. If it doesn't, her hope is that it will play a small part in guiding you there.

Julia Parks

Reflections

As we reached the end of her first coaching session, I saw my new client as if she and I were somehow intertwined. Her story was interlocked with mine, connected by our gender of womanhood and perhaps something far deeper I had yet to discover. The bravado of her body, boldly feigning strength she did not feel, the heated stream of tears falling from her eyes as she fought to contain them, and the shaking vibrational tone in her voice said it all: "I am broken. I am flawed. I am not enough. Yet here I am, still fighting."

There it was. The raw, brutal mental vomit of a mantra drilled into our subconscious from the foundation of our earliest years of life. Each repetitive asking of "Am I enough?" reinforced the inner dialogue, the questioning of our own significance, value, and place in the world. The same question asked multiple times over billions of women's lives challenges us to recognize that *we have chosen to stay in the fight*.

This woman before me was a mirror of my own fears—a reflection of all the degrading self-talk I had once accepted, based on a multitude of life experiences for which I held contempt. I viewed myself as incapable of conquering anyone or anything. I saw myself tangled in the grasp of inadequacy that was impossible to escape.

Yet, like her, I had chosen life. I had chosen to keep fighting to change the words on an invisible page. She and I were female warriors found on a battlefield in a chapter of our own books, taking on conquests and contrasts with unseen ferociousness and determination, often found in the shadows, hidden behind closed doors in our personal and professional lives. We were being tempered through our trials, honed to accept the exquisite power being unearthed within us. We were sisters battling to break free from the expectations forced upon us by the world we inhabit.

Sitting with my client, she became a beacon of light illuminating the darkness of aching memories stored in the fissures of my soul. The past pains, traumas, and abuses from which I had spent years healing became glowing scars sitting in plain view on my skin for all to see, if they were willing to look past the smile I wore to distract them.

Her words illuminated something far more despairing than pain. She made me hear my own screams of regret each time I had chosen to play small, to shrink back in terror, to hide from my fullest potential. There they were, standing before me: the regrets, my opponents in the battle that is still waging, even while I struggle to make find peace.

The world had not let me down; it owed me nothing. In a brief moment of introspection, I took in all that I had done to myself. My battle with my regrets was waged more fiercely than my conflict with the world. I was defeated by the overpowering message that *I would never be enough*. I had been both the heated adversary in *The Book of Julia* and the greatest advocate and heroin. I've been writing this story for over fifty years.

If I were to go into my accounts of childhood sexual traumas conducted by faux protectors from age two to thirteen or tell the story of the four-year-old me who would be fifty years old before she understood she was a warrior who could stand up to the predators, would that story touch you? Or the story about how, in my tender preadolescent years, I was groomed to be married at fourteen to my father's best friend, trapped in a life in which escape meant potential death, and staying meant enduring unsurmountable abuses. Would the story be more palatable if I told you I was absolutely resolute that *I would not be broken by him*?

Would such a story resonate with you? Or the later story of multiple medical experiences resulting from a paternal genetic disorder that kept surgery staff on standby for my children, or how the next emergency aortic surgery would leave me a widow, my children fatherless. I could try to convey the grief associated with the death of my second husband and the father of my five adult children, or how, as a result of his dying, both he and I found some relief? If I shared my experiences detailing the excruciating depths of depression, the paralyzing effects of CPTSD (Complex Post-Traumatic Stress disorder), and the struggles associated with trying to live with Dissociative Identity Disorder, all while pretending to be normal, would you be repelled? Inspired? Perhaps I could reveal the intimate and heart-wrenching battles that required me to become my own most fierce advocate as I faced healing from a medication-induced stroke the last three years of my life, would this touch you in a meaningful way?

Would you read that story? Would it make a difference? Details might be riveting, or spark curiosity, but that story would still not wholly contain what I and my sister travelers have experienced. It is the voice that rose from inside me during every encounter that matters. It is the voice that screamed louder than any pains endured. The voice of a toddler who matured into a woman who would not be silenced as she boldly cried out, "I AM CHOOSING LIFE!"

Such stories come to us all in one form or another. None of us are exempt from life's enigmatic persistence to draw us out of our depths of despair and fling us into growth, renewal, recovery. In truth, there is nothing uniquely special or significant about any of our stories, except how we have chosen to navigate them, how each disparity, loss, and tragedy has aided in the development of who we are as women, and how we choose to allow each one to empower the voice we speak within ourselves.

It is that voice, that gloriously resilient cry, that calls us to endure what we thought we could not. It is the intrinsic instinct that has propelled us into making a choice to thrive, well beyond the limited concept of survival. It is the recognition in my own life that I have the power to choose how and if I will hold a space for my life's magnificent, messy melodramas, mysteries, and masteries. It is the acceptance of who I am that accentuates my strengths. Mine is a powerful battle cry: "THIS IS WHO I AM!"

My voice is resonant, like many before me. It rises out of vulnerability, escapes from the bottomless terror, and shouts, "I CHOOSE I choose softness, love, gratitude, and joy. I accept opportunities revealed in open wounds to help instruct my soul.

We have chosen to not be hardened by our sufferings. We have adapted and created a path on our individual journeys, paths paved with unimaginable strength and fortitude. We are relentless in our resilience.

I do not pretend to speak for every woman reading these pages, but I hope my words connect with you. If I could pour a small amount of hope's light into you that would inspire you to see your worth . . . if I could help you find and feel the source of your most heartfelt power and encourage you to trust yourself as you live your story with newly formed intentionality, then perhaps these words from my life will offer up a legacy and make our journeys more fulfilling for having shared them.

I was told we either suffer from the disciplines required to live life to the fullest now or life's regrets will cling to our tongues when we eventually close our eyes in death. If this has any truth to it, then our time to live fully out loud with purpose and without abandon is now. When I transition into death, let the words clinging to my tongue be of absolute assurance that I fulfilled my purpose in the face of adversity! I am the writer of my story.

The session with my client was a reflection of the perceptions of truth I hold inside. My words are an offering to you to seek your truth and shout with a joy-filled voice as you choose to be who you are. It can be done.

The connection between the heart, mind, and soul has led Julia Parks on a deep and abiding journey to seek answers that bring about meaningful and fulfilling purpose. Through the process of accepting and surrendering to the teachers found in the darkness, she is able to embrace the precious Light. Heart-Centered Therapeutic Coaching was birthed as Julia's modality to assist others in their own healing.

She is the proud mother of five adult children, and Grammy J to her new grandson. In the process of reclaiming her own identity and affirming the calling to surrender to her own journey through life, Julia has chosen to change her last name to Caton, her maiden name, in order to create a new legacy for a name that once held much trauma. She has spent the last five years focusing on mental health, wellbeing, and spiritual guidance. She has an undergraduate degree in Human Development and a graduate degree in Human Relations with a focus on Mental Health. She currently offers Therapeutic Coaching, Spiritual Guidance, Transformation Tissue Therapy, and Level 2 Reiki, and she is an aspiring author.

www.facebook.com/julia.parks.16/

Tammy Thomas

Why I Survived

It was 2010 and I was an alcoholic. My children were supposed to go to my late husband's grandma's for the week. I was too drunk to make the trip, so my second husband took my children to my late husband's grandma's. He left them with her for a week of Bible school. He probably told her I was sick. I continued to drink that day until I blacked out. I woke up alone in the dark. I had slept through the remainder of daylight. Alone with myself. It was a scary place to be. As I looked around at my dark, disheveled living room, I asked myself, "Why? What is it all for? Why did I survive sexual abuse at my father's hands? Why did I deserve to spend my childhood waking up under my abuser's roof?"

I can accept and admit my father molested me in the bathtub when I was three-to-six years old. My sister was in the bath as well, and even at that early age, I protected her by offering myself. I was never safe, never. The molestation stopped when I was seven and my mother divorced my father, but then she reconciled and we all lived together until I was seventeen. I was never touched again.

As I sit here writing this, I realize how deeply this transgression affected me. It was the start of a pattern that stayed with me for the next forty years. The only way I could quit running away from myself was to mentally return and rescue that three-year-old girl. But before I could do that, I had to quit rescuing everyone else. That was my pattern—to help anyone and everyone. It was/is my drug. *If I am doing for others, I am earning my keep. If I am sacrificing myself, I am good.* That is a truly fucked-up message, that I am only worthy if I am sacrificing myself. Offering my body during those early years resulted in a negative relationship with how I felt and saw myself. My body was good if it protected people. It was bad if it made people do bad things.

My protection was to carry an extra thirty-five to forty pounds from age twenty to thirty-one. Being overweight offered a layer of protection, like a snowsuit when it is snowing. The more weight I carried, the more numb I could be. I started carrying extra weight after I was date-raped the second time in two years, resulting in pregnancy. I was eighteen and did not believe abortion was an option. I found myself alone on my grandma's couch praying, "God, why did you let this happen?" The answer I got from God was to make something beautiful out of something horrible. I contacted the Baptist children's home. I carried the baby to term. I chose his parents. He was born on the Fourth of July 1990.

I attempted suicide at twenty-seven. I did not want to hurt anymore so I took all my anti-depressants. My husband called his grandma. Grandma called the pastor. The pastor and the pastor's wife picked Grandma up. They came as fast as they could and rushed me to the ER at St. John's hospital in Tulsa. I drank charcoal. My stomach was pumped. I spent a few days in the psych ward wondering why I survived my suicide attempt.

Which led me to asking why I'd survived my first marriage, which was ten years of a physically abusive relationship. We had gone almost two years without an instance of abuse. I thought I had convinced him I would leave if he ever laid hands on me in anger again. The morning he killed himself, he had gotten physical with me for what would be the last time. He wanted me to fix his breakfast. I was supposed to be going to my college algebra final review at Tulsa Community College where I was taking my prerequisite and corequisite classes for the nursing program. I had 3.9 GPA. I had to go to the algebra review. I started getting dressed to leave for class.

He said, "Where are you going? Are you leaving me?"

I said, "My algebra review. I am not leaving you. I can't."

He was angry and threatening.

"If you touch me in anger, you will not be touching me in any other way again," I said, then added, "We will figure this out."

He left and came back with a shotgun.

I said, "What are you going to do? Kill me?"

He said, "No. The kids need you." Then he put the shotgun in his mouth and pulled the trigger. This six-foot-two, two-hundred-ten-pound, thirty-two-year-old man crumpled to the ground, his blood spraying on the wall and ceiling. My two-year-old daughter was in her high chair with a donut. Thank God she was in the high chair. I got a towel to put under what was left of his head. One of his eyeballs was hanging out of his skull. His breathing became labored, gasping, agonal. I still hoped he would be OK. I envisioned months of rehab. It was December 3rd, 2002. My daughter would turn two in eleven days. Christmas was just around the corner; I did not have time for him to be in rehab. I picked up the cordless home phone and called 911.

The ambulance, driven by a female ambulance driver, arrived quickly. She helped me get my daughter out of her high chair. She helped me gather clothes. She helped the sheriff test my hands for gunshot residue. I was pissed. How dare they think I would hurt him. She made sure I had a phone. I called my best friend Kelly and told her about the gunshot residue test. She said I needed to cooperate, that it was for my own good. It was to prove my innocence.

Kelly came immediately. She went with me to the church to get the pastor to go tell my husband's grandma he was gone. She took me to her house. She called my doctor for me. She took care of me for a few days. I survived. A few months later, I fell asleep at the wheel on my way home to Grandma's from a friend's house. I was ejected from the truck I was driving, then life-flighted to St. Francis Hospital in Tulsa. Although there would be many times I made the choice to see the beauty in trauma, this day wasn't one of them, at least not immediately. The head injury threw me for a loop. I was foggy, but I began healing.

The light I found at the end of that tunnel was that I needed to rest, reset, quit running. It was in this period I met and married my second husband. We have been together for nineteen years, and he is my best friend. We have had a lot of growing to do through the years. We had to grow both as a unit and as two completely separate autonomous beings. It has not been easy. He has been my constant, which is especially valuable to me, as I am not accepted by my family.

Back to waking up alone in my disheveled living room that held the remnants of my children's things—that was the thing that changed my life. I decided there had to be a purpose for my suffering. I decided there was no way I could have lived through all the trauma I'd survived up to this point to only become an addled alcoholic.

I decided I had five beautiful children and a husband who deserved better than I was giving. I decided to accept some love and acceptance from others. I decided I was going to find my purpose. I spent the next few days making better rules for myself; the most important was that I would wake up every day and do something to make the lives of three people better. They could be big things or little things; they could be strangers, family, or friends. It needed to be three things I chose to do. It needed to make someone's life a little easier, a little brighter.

This was how I transitioned. I knew I could no longer isolate and hide, that I had to stop sinking into the mud of my own pain. Running and numbing were my favorite escapes, and it was truly time to stop.

The world needed me. I began to look for the good in people. I quit drinking. I began to see the ripple effects of my three acts of kindness. My life began to change. I began to manifest opportunities. I manifested tickets for my husband and myself to UPW Dallas 2014.

The Dickens Process, a Neuro Linguistic Programming (NLP) technique, had a huge impact on me. It helped me look ahead at my life and realize that if I made no changes, it was clearly a dead end. So instead, I envisioned myself as the high school soccer star I had once been. I envisioned myself in a beautiful brick home on a hill. I envisioned myself a bestselling author. I envisioned myself happy, healthy, and ready to help others live their best lives.

I lost one hundred pounds and have been maintaining my weight for a few years. I continue to heal and grow and change into the best current version of me. Using Viome® testing, I learned my cellular age is forty-one. I am fifty. Not only have I lost one hundred pounds, but I have also learned to love and accept myself completely. I have learned I am enough. I live in that beautiful brick home on the side of a hill. I am using the knowledge and wisdom I learned on my journey to help others live their best lives. Did I mention becoming a bestselling author? My life has never been the same. It all started with a simple decision to find the beauty in my suffering, which enabled me to survive so I could heal out loud and show others how to do the same.

Tammy Thomas • Why I Survived

Tammy Thomas is a fifty-year-old mother of five. She is an observer and giver of wisdom, beauty, and love, a healer, a nurturer, and a loving soul. An accomplished cook and winner of recipe contests, Tammy co-owns LvnmyDrm LLC and House on the Hill produce and bakery. She owns Reflections Life Health and Wellness and is the creator of Women Unite. Tammy does these things because abuse happens at all ages and takes many forms. Even when the direct abuse ends, the effects remain. We have a responsibility to abused women and children to help them break free of the cycle. It is not their fault they are being or have been abused, that they don't know there are alternatives or haven't been shown how to carry on and build something beautiful when they finally break free. It is the fault of society allowing it to happen, of each of us turning our heads for fear of getting involved and of being glad it isn't us. Tammy's commitment is that, from this day forward, it *will not* be our fault that there is no support when and long after we've decided we are worth loving. The most important job she has is to continue healing out loud. Because of her, others can find their way to the light.

www.facebook.com/tammy.inmanthomas
www.facebook.com/womenunite2015
www.facebook.com/reflectionslifehealthandwellness
www.facebook.com/LvnmyDrm
lvnmydrm.com/
customerhappiness@lvnmydrm.com
Instagram @tammygg33
www.youtube.com/channel/UCJZMxe6ADNI70MbG_wV7WMA

Kristen Salvo

You Can't Pour From an Empty Cup!

In oneself lies the whole world, and if you know how to look and learn, then the door is there and the key is in your hand. Nobody on earth can give you either that key or the door to open, except yourself.

-Jiddu Krishnamurti

Growing up, I was there for anyone and everyone whenever they needed me. I wanted to gain acceptance. I thought this is what I had to do to ensure I had a circle of support around me. This people-pleasing behavior was a coping mechanism I developed when I was ten and lost my mom.

Friday afternoon on May 21st, 1999, I walked out of school and found my neighbor was there to pick me up instead of my mom. I immediately felt a knot in my stomach. Pulling up to her house, I saw my aunt's van with my sister and aunt inside. I wasn't close to my aunt, and she rarely came out to our house, so I knew something was wrong. They immediately embraced me and said that they wanted to take me to the park. Worried about my mom and wanting to get to camp on time, I didn't want to go to the park. But I had no choice. The drive to the park was a bit of a blur, but the words out of my aunt's mouth saying that my mother had passed away will never be forgotten. Finding out that my mom used the rope on my list to end her life felt like a horrible punishment, like I was the reason she did what she did. So much so, my body spasmed. It was too painful to face, so I buried my shame along with my grief.

I kept that shame barricaded inside. I decided to act strong. I lived in this this state of dysfunction for twenty years, disassociated with myself. I basically lived for other people, concealing my real feelings because I thought if anyone saw that I was broken, they would leave me like my mom had, and how my dad had chosen the bottle over his family when I was three years old. When our mother passed, my sister and I were taken to my aunt's house. It was a safe, stable place to live, but the emotional support I needed was not provided. My aunt did the best she could with what she knew, but she wasn't my mom. I did everything to get her to love and support me like my mom had, but what I didn't know then was that was impossible. She wasn't my mom.

Feeling lost and alone, I devoted my life to doing things for others to fill the void from my mother's absent love and support. I had not fully processed her death, so I was still searching for her. This isn't the way to process and heal, but it did lead me to surprising relationships and experiences, including some that did not serve me. My natural inclination was to choose codependent people because that seemed to be the safest way to open my heart. Or so I thought!

This took me down a dark, lonely, and painful path, but I now know *it was the path I needed to take* so that I could speak up for other people-pleasers and guide them to find themselves, teach them that always doing for others means getting to know them better than you know yourself.

The beginning of 2020, I hit rock bottom. I had been on my journey since 2013, unconsciously choosing toxic environments and people, thinking that was how to survive. It sucked all the healing, light, and love out of me. I ended things with a man who I thought I would marry. He had a son, who I already thought of as my stepson. I learned a lot about myself with this man, but he hadn't done healing work himself, so he projected his trauma onto me and was unable to open up. Breaking up with him reinforced the feeling that "I am not enough." I didn't know yet that I had to accept myself *as enough* before others could see it in me.

The same week of my breakup, I found out I had the pandemic virus. This meant lying in bed alone with my thoughts for three solid weeks. I'd never sat with myself that long. This is when I realized I not only needed help but that I also needed to be 100 percent devoted to my healing.

Getting off the people-pleasing wheel, I found that I was a lost soul and had a lot of work to do. The first thing I did was book a trip to Sedona after I received an invite from a tribe whom I had sat with before to do Ayahuasca.[2] Arizona was never on my list of places to visit, but I was pleasantly surprised when I arrived in Sedona. So much so, my body trembled. I felt as if I were home. I knew big changes were coming.

Going into Ceremony

I needed an intention to enter into Ayahuasca ceremony. I knew intuitively that this was the time to fully surrender to deep healing, and that without an intention, I would not be able to fully receive. I would hold back because of fear. My intention was to see *all of myself.* That is exactly what I received: deep ancient wisdom and clear connections to the spiritual world. I learned that we have to release fear in order to take risks, and risks must be taken in order to change.

Able in ceremony to clearly see and communicate spiritually with my mother, she showed me a Native American doll that she left for me and its location in my home. When I returned home, I went to the bin she showed me, and there, right on top, I found the doll. The doll and all that was in that bin confirmed my intention to figure out who I truly am and to find my soul's purpose.

---

[2] A tropical vine native to the Amazon region, noted for its hallucinogenic properties.

Higher Realms and Earthly Support

My mother is with me, and I speak to her every day. We all have angels around us, but we must *ask* in order to receive. There is a higher realm. Those who don't believe this don't understand *that we are spiritual beings having a human experience, not humans having a spiritual experience* (Pierre Teilhard de Chardin).

The path to enlightenment can be much more fun when you have a supportive tribe, but first I had to completely isolate myself and start from the bottom. Loneliness is dark energy. To clear it means realizing you are never alone. In my mother's death note that was in the bin, she wrote that she didn't want to go but she didn't know the meaning of life anymore. She was a loving, kind, giving woman who endured abuse on so many levels. She knew this abuse could happen to me, and by leading me to the bin, she invited me to break the chain, move out of the darkness and into the light. *My purpose is to show others it is possible.* I am not my trauma, my body, or my status in this world. I am a soul here on assignment to bring light to others. Anyone or anything that gets in the way, I detach from with love.

Detaching

My detachment process was very difficult. I had to make hard choices and separate from friends and close family, but I remembered my intention and vision and knew I was ready to elevate to something greater. The healing journey has ebbs and flows, highs and lows that must be embraced to fully heal. *Things happen for us, not to us* (Sam Liebowitz). So if your best friend doesn't call you anymore because you no longer bend over backward to help her out, it isn't a loss; it is a chapter in your life that has come to an end. Separating yourself from all you thought you needed may seem challenging, but detaching from people, places, things, and outcomes is the most freeing thing you can do for yourself . . . and it the way to elevate to something higher.

Getting Off Track

Your life path is already planned, and it is up to you to take the high road every moment of every day in order to stay on track. If you get off track, don't sweat it. You were meant to get off track to learn a lesson. Whatever arises, find the light and lesson needed to grow. Don't get caught up on *why*, *how*, or *if*. You can get back on track with a simple shift in your perception to find the lesson, then embody the change required for you to *grow*. The key is to get back on track as quickly as possible.

Stepping Into the Unknown, Diving Into Fear

After returning from my trip to Sedona, I felt a shift in my energy. When I was there, I felt seen, heard, and supported by the people and the land. I cried when I left the first time, and missed it so much I went back six times in eight months. When I realized that the business I had built for six years, the house of my dreams, and the people around me didn't define me, I decided that it was in my highest and best interest to follow my heart and step into the unknown.

One year after my first arrival in Sedona, I returned to become a full-time resident. This was an experiment in total surrender. I'd sold my house fully furnished and drove across country in my motorhome. This was not what others thought I should do, as you can imagine, but the call I felt in my soul was so clear, no one could convince me to stay. I lost some people, I gained some people. I saw life from my perspective instead of theirs. Diving into fear enabled me to find myself, surrounded by loving support, and live in a home better than I had envisioned.

Soul Work

Soul work is my full-time job. When I focus on that, everything else falls into place. Opportunities and connections of a lifetime have been presenting themselves since releasing control of my journey and completely surrendering to my intuition. That's what life is all about. It was time to fill my cup in order to have the time, space, and energy to do for myself what I had done for others since I was ten years old. This is called self-care. I didn't learn about self-care in my family because it was viewed as being selfish. In reality, you cannot fill another's cup in an authentic way if your cup is empty. Filling others' cups when you don't have a full one yourself is a form of codependency, which is not only an unhealthy way to live but also the perfect potion for brewing resentment toward others.

So how did I reunite with my soul? Healing isn't a one-size-fits-all option. You can try what worked for others to see if that resonates with you. I also believe you must go on your own quest and find your own tools. I call all of my healing modalities "tools," and I wear my tool belt each day in case something arises and I need to recenter with my sweet soul and its purpose here on Earth. Your soul path offers love, acceptance, healing, abundance, and freedom. You have lessons to learn, which create opportunities to both go within and reach out to your support team in order to grow. Support is a key ingredient for growth. You must have at least one person in your life who is unbiased, loving, supportive, and also walking down their soul path.

In Summary

Do the work. Embrace aloneness as an opportunity to heal and learn more about yourself. Speak to the spiritual realm, give them permission to connect, and open your heart with trust. Know that you're not alone. Be vulnerable and find support that aligns you with your dreams. Lastly, and most importantly, *you are not in control.* Release control so God can intervene and continue his plan for you. I have the most profound experiences when I say this simple prayer:

God, my guides, my angels, and all spiritual beings of love and light, please forgive me for trying to control my life. Please intervene and continue with your perfect plan. I ask you to fill me with strength and love to move forward. I am ready to receive.

Thank you. I love you!

Life is on your side, and you are deeply loved and protected. *Never* forget that.

Kristen Salvo • You Can't Pour From an Empty Cup!

Kristen Salvo started her still-successful career as an entrepreneur when she was eighteen years old, her drive fueled by fear. In 2013, a traumatic experience motivated her to search for life's deeper meaning. Her quest has taken her to jungles where she drank Ayahuasca with indigenous tribes, to silent meditation where she spent thirty days with world-renowned leaders, and to countless hours spent with life coaches, after which she applied her laser-beam focus on nutrition and exercise. With a burning desire to help others on this journey, she learned alternative healing modalities outside the Western approach, applying them first to heal her deep wounds and then to teach others how to turn *fear into fuel and obstacles into opportunities*. A #1 international best-selling author, she resides in Sedona, Arizona, and believes that a balanced life of faith, support, love, and passion are the ingredients needed to manifest a life beyond our wildest dreams.

www.facebook.com/kristen.salvo.5
www.kristensalvogroup.com

Heidi Cecil

I'm Just Getting Started

Angst. You know that feeling you get when someone asks you to take on a new challenge? Yup, that's the one. You say maybe. You are going to "think about it." You get a little breathless as you think about how you can possibly add anything else to your plate. You've already run through your mental checklist of the day before this task came up, and you were already overwhelmed.

You must be out of the house before seven a.m. to get your child to school, get your work done with meetings and appointments, and who even has time for lunch? Work never goes as planned. There will be a client who has an emergency. Or all of them will. You can't do this. You must make it to the bank and the post office. Your dog seemed a little sick last night. You haven't picked up your groceries. Your emails are piling up. You're never going to catch up on laundry, and when was the last time anyone dusted? It's time for the cat's check-up, among another million things.

The anxiety starts to overwhelm you. You can't do this. As you move through your day you feel like it's going to be too much. Does anyone even understand what you have going on in your life? Why were you asked to do this? Wasn't anyone else available? You take a deep breath. You have been here before. You know what to do. You know inside you've got this! But shit! Your daughter is out of school. Did you have someone pick her up? You can't do this. How is it so late already? What is wrong with you?

How did you…wait, the orthodontist is calling to confirm your child's appointment tomorrow. You forgot to write that down when they called you to change it last week. Now you have a conflict as drivers ed is also scheduled.

That beautiful child sails through the door with a smile that lights up the room as you end that phone call. You realize you can stop holding your breath. You have things in place to make life go right even if you miss a beat. You get a text that someone backed out of a project you are working on. Smile. Girl, you've still got this. It's one of the most joyful things you've done. That next thing you were asked to do? Oh no. Back to that old feeling. I can't. How can you? You didn't even have it together enough to know if your daughter was picked up at school.

Panic. Your heart is going too fast. Your hands start to sweat. You can't get your thoughts to organize. Breathe. Nope. Hold your breath. Like you do. Why is this happening? You feel the heat behind your eyelids, a familiar burn. It's in your soul. Why are you crying? Did you hit send on that last email for your client? Did you drink enough water today? The tears start to fall. Drinking water makes you cry now? How are you actually a grown-up? Where is your responsible adult? You cry harder. You can't do this. You have never done this before.

You take a minute to wash your face and make sure you look like someone you would want to do business with again. You feel shaky and anxious. You look in the mirror. At your own reflection in your own eyes. You see the doubt and the hesitation. The fear. You know the things you are doing are right for your life. You know the changes are amazing and powerful and that everything aligns as it should, when it should. You know lives are being changed every day for the better. Your favorite banker calls. She knows you are a little overwhelmed right now. She has your back. Stop sweating. You didn't accidentally transfer all your money to some unknown account out of the country. She says, "Your last DocuSign was incomplete, I sent it back." She gives you details on what to do. Exactly. Like a child. you are holding up your own transaction. You better say no. You can't do this. You need a responsible adult.

Your brain races about that next challenge. You know it matters and you know you want to do it. How can you get it done? How can you fit it in? Nope! You just saw that girl in the mirror. You looked in her eyes and saw a hot mess. You saw how she couldn't get a document signed properly and—wait, did you check to see if you ever hit send on that last email? Oh, you have to leave in five minutes to get your daughter to work, and why is this happening? Why can't you get your brain to hold all the information and not get overwhelmed? All these family and life events swirl through your head and you remember the place you came from. The people around you. You seriously can't do this. You better call and say no. You'd do an amazing job, but you can't let them down and you don't want to embarrass yourself. You call to say no. After all, look at your life. You're busy. She will understand.

Stop, girl! Stop!

I made that call to say no and said yes. First word out of my mouth. I couldn't contain it. It wasn't even my choice, really. A friend recently asked me if something paid me enough in joy to continue. She knows that's my thing. I realized that's how I've been making decisions. I just couldn't put the words to it. I went from a "No, I can't" girl to a "Hell yes, let's do this" girl.

Deliberately. By design.

I allowed racing thoughts and anxious feelings to push and pull me for one day. All day. It wasn't about that next challenge. It was about limiting beliefs. It was about getting in my own way. It was about sadness, old habits and behaviors (that shit is hard to break. Ugh!), and frustrations about changes that I still don't handle with as much grace as I'd like.

I used to let all that negative self-talk and fear stop me. I just (mostly) stayed in my lane and didn't really do anything that caused that level of anxiety. I was so boring! My life was awful. "No" is easy. I wasn't growing as a person, and I was unhappy. I'd said no out of a fear of failure, and still I failed. I said no for silly reasons like "What if they don't like me? What if I'm not good enough, not smart enough, not *enough*?"

Let's stop right there. I'm forty-nine and I'm just getting started.

I *am* enough! I am worthy. I trapped myself in worry. I worried about others' opinions, even my own opinion of what their opinion might be. I let that stop me from saying yes too. This is how I went from "no" to a Yes Girl.

What? Screw fear! I'm enough! I may fail. I'm going to make my dream happen. Somehow! I'm more scared of ending up on a couch watching TV every night and whining about what I see in the news all day.

So I spent a whole day lost in "not enough." The good news these days is I usually don't lose a whole day. A few hours or minutes are normal. At least it didn't cost me forty-seven freaking years again! I missed opportunities I wish I had taken. I only have this one life. I'm living it full on for the rest of it!

I've surrounded myself with an amazing tribe of beautiful people who support and love me, and I feel the same about them. We all connect and align on thoughts and life. I lean on them when I have my conflicted "It's all too much, I'm not enough" days. And when I'm just plain joyful.

I was talking to my best friend about this recently, about my lapse into negativity and fear. She wouldn't let me play the game. She knows me. She called me out, with love. I didn't want to call her because I knew we would have a conversation I really didn't want to have. I've known her forever, and we've had plenty of tough conversations with each other. I know she's the person in my tribe I need to call because she won't let me get away with shit. She handles me with grace. She is not the friend I call if I want to be coddled through a problem I need to solve. Together, we handle the real stuff.

My tribe supports my yeses—and my noes, when it's the better response. I cannot imagine life without them. They give me absolute joy. They are the people I call my responsible adults. They are family by blood or choice. They keep me in line, they think positive, they say yes! They love and shine their light in the world in a way that can't be dismissed, and I am proud of each of them, of myself. I surround myself with a tribe that humbles, inspires, and adds the best joy, magic, and laughter to my life. This is what I give in return. I love being that for them. They are my dream team!

I invite you to find your tribe and pull them close in moments of fear, indecision, and joy. We weren't meant to handle the world alone. Your tribe will embrace you, lift you up, and do it with glorious human imperfection.

Heidi Cecil • I'm Just Getting Started

Heidi Cecil is delightfully engaged in starting a new venture, campgroundtbd, with her business partner. Campgroundtbd is fulfilling her dream of helping others learn to live a joyful life. She is currently in the process of moving from the Oklahoma City metro area to the most beautiful mountain in Southeast Oklahoma. Heidi spent the last two years transforming her body, mind, and spirit to embrace the value of self-love. She now enjoys working with others to do the same. An international best-selling author, she continues to write, and she loves to assist clients seeking the perfect insurance solution at the Wood Agency in Bethany. Heidi has three children she is extremely proud of and loves to spend time with: Drew, age twenty-six; Kaylee, age twenty-four; and Hannah, age sixteen.

www.facebook.com/Heidi.cecil11
www.facebook.com/camptbd
Wood Agency OKC | Knock on Wood. We're here to help.

Jen Zoë Hall

Beautifully Broken

If you've ever seen the American Super Bowl, you've probably seen a Budweiser Clydesdale. And for some of you, the commercials with that cute little Golden Retriever and the glorious Clydesdale that loves him might still bring tears to your eyes. Even now as I write this, I can hear the music and feel the emotion when the two are reunited at the end of a story that has nothing to do with beer! When I think back to my earliest childhood memory as a little towheaded blonde, I too had an experience with a Clydesdale that would plant a seed in my soul, although as a four-year-old, I had no idea how deep.

Almost forty-four years later I still recall the encounter with startling clarity. It was 1978, and I was with my mother, my hand in hers as we walked out of the IGA grocery store in my hometown of Poplar Bluff, Missouri. As we walked toward our wood-paneled station wagon, I noticed a large tent in the back of the parking lot. Now that was not particularly interesting, but what walked out of it a few moments later most certainly was. You see, like most little girls, I was obsessed with horses. I played with toy horses for hours in the basement and even had a model barn instead of the standard dollhouse.

I tugged on my mother's hand to go and see the majestic creatures, and of course she knew it was futile to argue. I remember how tall they were, but I also remember that I wasn't afraid. I strode up to the groom handling them and tugged on his pant leg. In a clear voice, I said, "Hey mister, can I ride your horse?" I don't remember his expression, but I can only imagine he had to chuckle at how certain I was he was going to say yes. He leaned down and gently explained that these were special horses and that they weren't for riding. My mother led me, crestfallen and sad, back toward the car and away from the horses.

Just as we were about to leave, a shiny truck pulled in and out piled a whole family. Father, mother, and, as luck would have it, a little girl about my age. You see, this was the family of the local Budweiser beer distributor coming to check on the upcoming event. With my crocodile tears flowing, I looked back one last time to say a longing goodbye to the horses, and I saw the groom picking the distributor's daughter up and putting *that* little girl on the back of one of the Clydesdales I'd been forbidden to ride.

My tears turned to howls of injustice. Why did that little girl get to ride and I did not? Who was she and why was she better than me to get a privilege that I had been denied? I fell in love with my mother in that moment, as we turned right back around and, oh yeah, you better believe I got to sit astride one of the most famous horses in the world that day. My little legs were almost as wide as my smile as I sat on his broad back, never wanting to come down or let go. Yes indeed, that day planted a seed a seed deep inside my soul.

It's funny how beliefs are planted, what lessons are learned and how they shape the stories we hold. As I grew older and went on with life, I never lost my love of horses, but life and survival became the focus. Doing what I was supposed to do and should do was what shaped my story. I could go into my childhood, where I was bullied by kids at school, disciplined harshly by teachers. Home life was the same. The rule at home was, if you got in trouble at school, you got in twice as much at home. For a seven-year-old extrovert, it was terrifying. That little girl who demanded justice for herself that day with the horses was being shaped into something very different by society and the system. I feared every day that I would do something wrong and get in trouble. That became my biggest fear, and the feeling of terror I had anytime I would get in trouble became something I would do anything to avoid.

By the time I graduated high school, I was a confused mess. I had been disciplined and threatened into getting good enough grades to get into college, and my intelligence alone had won me some scholarships, but I was lost. I had no idea what I wanted or wanted to do. I had no real life skills, no friends, and I felt completely isolated. I would put out to any boy who made me feel like I had even a glimmer of a chance of being loved. Unfortunately, the definition of love I grew up with came with the baggage of abuse and manipulation.

College was one of the hardest times in my life. I was arrested twice, incurred tens of thousands of dollars in debt, and spent almost seven years of hell to get a piece of paper I had no idea why I needed or what it would do for me. I hated college, every last minute of it, but fear of my father's wrath and disappointment kept me on a path that I felt offered me no choice. Multiple feeble attempts at suicide checkered my college experience, but finally, in 1998, I managed to graduate and get married, following yet again my father's vision of what life should be for me.

I spent the next several years trying to make my job work, fighting with the man I was supposed to love, and self-medicating to cope. Feeling isolated, the days blurred together. Every day was mediocre shade of beige.

Then, on July 31st, 2004, something snapped. My husband was gone and I found myself shampooing the carpets in my house in the middle of the night, binge-drinking and watching old movies, filling the time and space with something to make me feel productive. As the sun rose over my fervent endeavor to make a perfect household, I looked around at the perfectly steamed carpets in an empty house and knew I needed to make a change. Call it divine guidance, but I woke up with the sunrise a quarter of a century after that fateful ride on a special horse and took the first step into a world that would change my life forever. I decided to quit smoking cigarettes and start taking horseback riding lessons.

Much of that part of my life flashes before me like the fleeting scenes on a train. I set goals that were for me and no one else, and glimpses of that little girl and her passion started to rise within me. I had dreams of going to the Olympics and being a champion. I seemed crazy to those who knew me. My family rolled their eyes at yet another of my crazy ideas. This time I didn't care or listen. I jumped in with a fervor I'd never had with any other endeavor. I read books, watched videos, and drove over an hour every week to get a lesson. I discovered a different side of horses, something that was outside the world of competition. It felt like I had discovered a unique version of Oz viewed through the beauty that horses could bring to my life.

The joy of getting my own first horse was almost surreal. I had been saving for what seemed like forever to buy a horse. We had decided to move to Florida, so my budget had dwindled, but, at the last minute, the planets aligned and I won a jackpot at a casino, just enough for me to buy Dante, a giant and fiery chestnut Quarter Horse that proved to be aptly named. After owning him for about two weeks, I realized I knew very little about actually owning horses. As it turned out, Dante had been severely abused and was dangerous in the hands of a virtual beginner. The learning curve was huge. I had been crying in my sleep when I woke up one morning, bruised and scared, thinking to myself, "If this is horses, I'm not sure I can do it."

But I stayed with it. I didn't feel like I could make a different choice. I got another horse and threw myself into working with both of them. I stayed the course and knew that there was no offer I was willing to accept in exchange for my dream, and I would pay any price to pursue it. The fire that stirred inside me kept burning.

I stayed in a loveless marriage and lived continuously in fear of how we were going to live. I was afraid if I tried to leave, I would lose my horses. I believed I had nothing of value to offer this world except what I had to support my husband. It sounds so foreign to say now looking back, but I had learned how to be helpless. Taught over time, it can be a tough lesson to break; however, in those moments the universe sometimes intervene.

The challenge when you are in chaos is that the intervention of the universe can be more like a chainsaw than a scalpel. My reliance on comfortability was so strong, the universe forced me to step into the unknown. So when I woke up to a message from a strange woman about my husband and how he was illegally financing our lifestyle, my life as I knew it was over in a flash.

It sounds cliché to say that I lost everything. I was without a home, a job, friends, and I had no real marketable skills. It was deeply humbling to go back to waitressing at nearly forty, but I wouldn't trade that part of the struggle, because what I learned was *the strength came through that struggle and that was worth it*. I discovered a natural form of horse training and began blending that with personal development. I tapped back into what was important to me and gave myself permission to be who I authentically was. I began to fall in love with myself, the adult version of that little girl who just loved horses.

I make no apologies for failures or choices that took me down the soul's path. My horses were the only thing in my life during that dark time that didn't judge me or have any expectations of me. I realized that I had been lied to my entire life, and until I connected with my own truth, I was only going to believe those lies.

Working with horses is no easy task. They are nature in its finest form. Forming the connections I had with them developed a side of me that I became proud of. I could tell the truth. I could see inauthenticity in others. I learned about boundaries and confidence and how to lead myself. I rediscovered my inner little girl and started to allow her to shine. I also learned how to love without judgement, develop growth, and learn with creativity and no rules.

I learned the feeling of freedom with something that loved me unconditionally and without judgement and I could love the same way in return. I released the self-doubt through connecting with my inner truth and, ultimately, I learned how to know myself, love myself, and believe in myself. It changed my life.

From a small town in Southeast Missouri, Jen Zoë Hall started her career with horses when she was thirty years old with aspirations of competing in the Olympics. Shortly into her journey with horses, she discovered a unique way to communicate with them and discovered her world of personal development. It was then she knew that there was way more to horses than just riding. After a devastating divorce, facing homelessness and losing her brother to a drug overdose, she began using her expertise in horses and self-help to create programs to empower and inspire women and veterans. A published author, speaker, and behavior expert, Jen Zoë now resides in West Palm Beach, Florida, and has spent the last eighteen years creating and developing The Zenerjen Method of Equine Assisted Empowerment Programs.

For more information about Equine Assisted Empowerment, visit her website at www.zenerjen.com or contact her team at hello@zenerjen.com.

www.facebook.com/Zenerjen
www.instagram.com/jenzoehall/
www.linkedin.com/in/jen-zoë-hall-5a914541/
www.youtube.com/zenerjen

Crystal Clenney

Listen Deeper

I *knew* death. I *knew* car accident. It felt like my own death, somehow, before it happened. More than six months of premonitions left me with the stark feeling I was going to, very specifically, die in a car accident. Precognizance, claircognizance…it goes by many names. I was clearly experiencing a psychic and kinesthetic *knowing*, beyond logic. It left me with a solid, undeniable *feeling-based knowing* of how I am leaving this world.

I am twenty-seven, living up north in Grand Rapids, and it's August, with autumn almost upon us. If you know Michigan at all, you know it's the rainy season just about then. I'm talking Thor's thunder with sheets of rain that pummel the ground for hours. They have whiteouts in the winter and washouts in the late summer.

For months I have been experiencing this *knowing beyond knowing*… this sense of inescapable impending doom. Somehow it feels like I have already been here; viscerally, I simply understand this feeling. I feel it in my skin. I'm so confused. This isn't real. I'm safe. I look around, check myself, my body, my face, my eyes. I'm here and now, not dead, not injured, not in any accident. I'm OK, I'm whole.

Still, this *knowing* invades my dreams, waking and sleeping, consuming my thoughts when working or driving or just walking and being. It's a completely pervasive feeling that I just can't shake, no matter what.

So strange. *Why* is this happening? Why is it so intense? I succumb after a time.

"Really, universe…that's how I'm gonna die? Is that why I've traveled so much so young, felt free and move fast like fury to do the things I've wanted to do, no matter what, no holds barred?"

Is it even possible to know how you're gonna die ahead of time? Why would I want to know that? Maybe it's better to know than not know? Or is it?

The day goes by, no accident. The next, the same. So I ask, "When is this accident going to happen? Can I know that at least?" A month goes by. No accident. Three months go by, still alive. Feelings persist, *knowing* becomes clearer.

A surrender is felt when clarity shines. A neutrality appears when clarity shows up. It's like the universal handshake, signaling a cosmic matter-of-fact moment. I spent months unable to reconcile this internal preview. I had to let it go. Lay it down and rest.

It's too much to *know* that, and yet to not know, how can I live with that?

More months pass. I've forgotten as much as possible about this looming feeling. I've pushed it hard to the outer edges of my gray matter, tucked it neatly away in the narrowest of chasms between my skull and tissue. A distant whisper still presents *when I pay attention.*

My alarm goes off. It's 4:30 a.m. in late August 2004. I set the alarm to wake up early for a thrilling playdate trip! I'm driving three hours to Six Flags in Chicago. I want to be there when the doors open! It's raining out, Michigan style. Still very dark…*darkest before the dawn*. Sheets and sheets of rain come down on Hwy 131 South. I can't see the end of my car.

Wondering if I should pull over or slow down, I decide to slow down and keep driving.

The wipers can't wipe fast enough. My heart is racing. What should I do? Maybe for real, pull over? I won't make it to Chicago in time if I wait this out. It could rain for hours, as it often does. I keep driving slowly, uncertain. I pull onto the next highway, then the next. I'm still not out of Grand Rapids proper. This is going to take a while.

My body is tense. *Breathe.* My hands white-knuckle the steering wheel, my speed reduced. I'm going to be late. Better late than never, I guess. I pull around a bend, merging onto a new highway. It's ever darker here.

"Wait! What's that?" I exclaim internally as a flash of a man appears in front of my moving vehicle. Something is ahead of me, but I can't make it out. I'm squinting. Rain is pelting my windshield so hard still…the fug! It looks like…what? It looks like I'm looking through windows?

I'm disoriented. This makes no sense at all. Why are windows right in front of me like that? I'm on the highway, still moving. Then all of a sudden, I see it. An SUV, sideways, perpendicular to mine, with no time to turn! No time to swerve, no time to escape. I hard steer all the way to the right. Instinct. Then *boom*! C.R.A.S.H. My car is stopped in this drenching darkness, on a multilane highway in downtown Grand Rapids. I keep thinking I better back up, move my car. Will it move? I scramble to collect my thoughts. Will someone hit me just like I hit this car?

I take in the scene. I'm in the middle lane of traffic. The right shoulder is open, maybe I should go there. Can I even get there? Do I physically get out? I assess further. Where's the man? There was a man! So confusing. I look to my left and see a small Ranger-size pickup truck on the left shoulder. I see a man banging fiercely on his steering wheel. He is so upset!

Seeing that driver's body moving, I check my own body—my face, my legs, my chest, my hands, arms. The airbags are not deployed. I'm wrecked, inside and out, but my actual body is OK. No visible damage there.

My hood is jacked. Bad front-end collision in the dangerous middle lane. Rain-smeared cars whiz by, spraying water trails as they pass. Three vehicles. Two drivers. Where's the third driver?

I put my car in reverse, relieved I can turn it on and put it in gear. I begin backing up my car, then *thump, thump* as my tires roll over something. My heart is pounding, now at the Speedy Gonzales level. I can't see what I rolled over.

"Shit, did I just roll over the guy? There was a guy, I saw him! Geezus!" I continue moving my car to the right shoulder.

No man in sight. I look to where I thump-thumped. There was a bumper. My relief is incomprehensible.

Who's bumper, though? Mine? OK, I'm safe in the right shoulder now. I get out, call 911. I grab my umbrella out of my trunk, then walk to the left shoulder. There is a man on the ground.

The pickup driver remains in his truck, still upset. His hood is now V-shaped.

The man on the ground has his blues on, with his four-letter embroidered name on his chest patch. Looks like he is a mechanic heading to work? I speak his name to him, holding the rain shield over him, inquire if he's OK while taking another assessment. There's a cut above his eyebrow. One of his arms is bent in a place that most definitely should not be bent. Swallowing my own shock, I console him and affirm help is on the way. Grunts are his only response, but he's conscious.

Not a scratch on me. Later, I learned there wasn't a scratch on the pickup driver. Police arrived, EMTs, the whole uniformed emergency crew. Investigations ensued, attorneys were assigned, depositions taken;

there was even a trial that lasted almost a decade. The man died after two weeks in the hospital.

That sudden flash of a man I saw through a torrential downpour was him running across the road, and while I steered right, there was a truck behind me that steered left. When the man ran left, the pickup's front end hit him directly.

For years afterward, I was constantly reminded of this incident when the base of my neck would swell from the whiplash injury, or when the benign dark and wet combined when I was behind a wheel, or when a random, sudden burst of memories would emerge without warning movie-style, playing scene-by-scene in my mind's eye.

Fifteen years later, I discovered an aspect that emerged in a conversation seemingly unrelated to this experience (as if that's ever true). I professed to my father my true passion and desire, that I had launched a new platform I developed called *Intuitive Human*©. Intuitive Human© excavates highly impactful, view-shifting intuitive experiences that go beyond logic and reason, creating an up-leveled human living life very differently. Intuitive Human© excavates the nuances of these experiences to identify trends and patterns among eighteen different tracks of intuition. We are taking this work to the leading edge of science, to include identifying biological measurements for intuition itself.

On this day with my father, I asked him if he ever had any strong intuition about *anything* in his life. He shared with me the only stand-alone experience he could recall because he doesn't really believe in "all that mumbo jumbo." When he was twenty-seven, he kept having a dream of his car being rolled off the side of a cliff. He felt like he was going to die. He was living in California at the time, stationed there while in the Navy. He described this dream as repeating itself night after night for about six months or so. "I couldn't shake it," he recalls.

Sure enough, one night he had too much to drink and was driving home when he found himself living out his dream. His pickup was rolling over a cliffside, just like his dreams showed him. He was inside, end over end, rolling down the mountainside. He crash-landed in a drunken stupor at the base of the cliff, against a tree...and somehow managed to walk away scratch-free, just like me.

For both my father and I to share similar premonitions, precognizance, these claircognizant dreams and kinesthetic feelings of imminent and inescapable death by car accident—shown to us ahead of time at the same age of twenty-seven—and neither of us ever having that dream again post-accident...had it instantly vanished or had it lived itself to completion?

I wondered at that moment how many coincidences it takes to be called to something more. I then shared my eerily mirrored experience with him, my body covered with goose bumps as I revealed my pre-incident intuitions and my accident. He was speechless at our shared "mumbo jumbo" experience that spanned decades. Learning this firsthand had me multidimensionally curious about questions I didn't even have the words for—questions about ancestral, generational intuitive experiences, karma, DNA and trauma, cellular memory, epigenetics, and more. How was any of this even possible? Truly.

This is what I live for! This is what I know: humans are rich with vast experiences, beyond knowing and believing. There are troves of treasure waiting to be opened, to be received, if we open to one another and never, never stop seeking.

It is time to ask the buried questions. We are effervescent beings, more connected and more the same than we are different. To you, the reader: be curious. Talk to your DNA, ask for its secrets, and then...Listen Deeper.

Crystal Clenney • Listen Deeper

Crystal Clenney is an international storyteller, public speaker, intuitive, empath, owner of an enterprise payroll software consultancy, a startup fractional CFO, and founder of a platform called Intuitive Human©. Crystal never looked back after being spontaneously awakened by a three-hour L.I.S.T.E.N. experience at age twenty-five, which she describes as "…lighted shards of glass entering and healing my body."

With her belief systems completely shattered, she began a focused mission to learn more about what happened, dedicating the next twenty years to studying energy medicine, natural healing, and cultivating and fine-tuning subtle levels of awareness. Today, Crystal excavates intuitive experiences globally, helping others unearth and integrate highly impactful, view-shifting intuitive events. Intuitive Human© discovers nuanced trends and patterns across eighteen intuitive tracks, defining the somatic signaling system and revealing how intuition is communicating in our bodies. Attuning to intuition is like tuning the human instrument to play the best song of your life.

intuitivehuman.com/herecomesthesun
intuitivehuman.com
www.instagram.com/intuitive_human/
www.facebook.com/crystal.clenney/
www.youtube.com/channel/UC0X09SWRjnderchd7_-Piow

Devie Richards

Life Beyond Borders

I'm not saying you should quit your job. What I am saying is that you can. I believe with my whole heart that you can have the life you want from nothing more than your own declaration. You aren't even required to keep the same declaration. You can change your mind and your life as often as you want. Don't believe me?

What if, for a little while today, you pretend to be anyone. I'll choose. You're Mother Teresa. Take a deep breath and embody the gentle tenderness of a woman you've never met. No matter what or whom you encounter, show up with love and compassion. Your words are kind, and your spirit calm. Without regard to outcome, you are love and acceptance. Perhaps you question whether God even exists, just as Teresa did; maybe you question yourself, but you return to center and exhale compassion. Nothing else matters until the experiment is over. You can tell yourself this is bullshit all you want…do it anyway. You can quit anytime, obviously, but why would you? This is nothing more than an exercise to show you how it feels to be anyone. Geeze, you could choose Lizzo or Ruth Bader Ginsberg. The point is, if you can act like someone else, why not make up who you want to be and become *her*?

I know this isn't "normal" conversation. Most people aren't sitting around listing and sharing out loud who they want to be. Instead, we do it inside the worst therapy office there is: our heads. This next line is not of my own creation, but it is priceless:

Your ego is not *your amigo*. The value of that six-word combination pales in comparison to your value and the vital role you play in a universe full of miracles. Stay out of your head. The value of that six-word combination pales in comparison to your value and the vital role you play in a Universe full of miracles. As a coach, I almost always begin a partnership by asking, "If you could have anything, what would it be?" Without question, the top answer has to do with money. "I want to be a multimillionaire. I want enough money to live comfortably and send my kids to college. I want to pay off (insert debts, loans, etc...)." So then I ask what they imagine it would feel like to have a bazillion dollars. Like if they closed their eyes, took a deep breath, and felt their "bazillionaireness," what's that like? What are their feelings? While people think they want a mountain of money (well, I mean, who doesn't?) the essence of what they're seeking is something besides actual dollar bills.

In 2005, I participated in the Landmark Forum. Three days and an evening opened my eyes to how I was and was not living my life. I looked at what happened and then what I made it mean. I saw how many of my so-called current conversations were carryovers of stories I made up in childhood and no longer serve me. I completed those conversations, and put them where they belong; in the past. I am the cause and the effect of my life. Life doesn't get to just happen to me. I consciously create how it goes. Words create World. And my word in FREEDOM. I get to say. As a matter o' fact, I now see what sets me apart is what I do say. Specifically, I say *Yes*!

I went to college in the eighties. We all said yes to lots of things, then; that's not what I'm talking about. I'm talking about saying yes to pulling over to take a picture of a view that takes your breath away; or saying yes to an invitation to a get-together where you may only know the hostess. I'm talking about saying yes to getting a passport so that you're ready to go anywhere in the world, and then picking up and going because you've always wanted to see blue-footed boobies, Machu Picchu, and think it's fun to tell people you went to Lake Titicaca. You could say yes to getting a bird feeder. There are *so* many ways to say yes. Yes, however, is not always rainbows and unicorns. You could say yes to being the companion and caretaker of a world-renowned author and actor, only to find that person behaves in the most disagreeable, cruel, narcissistic ways imaginable. So, despite your star-struck, giddy yes, you can stand for yourself and others and in no uncertain terms terminate your relationship effective immediately. *Sometimes yes means saying no.*

In 2010, fifteen years into a teaching career, I turned in my resignation. (I literally wrote my resignation on a piece of paper and handed it to my boss.) People were surprised but not really. I had a pile of bills and ten thousand dollars my dad had gifted me. I quit an itchy-sweater-albeit-steady-paycheck job, and though I say I didn't have a plan, I did. I bought a plane ticket and showed up in South America. That was my plan. I didn't research the weather or hotels or when things were open. For three months, I walked, rode, ate, and did what I wanted. I lugged my suitcase around Ecuador, Peru, Bolivia, and the Galápagos; visited World Heritage sites; discovered Ayahuasca, cuy, and pisco sours; and excelled at my imbedded-fly by-the-seat-of-my-pants way of being. There I was. Traversing borders. Not just the imaginary lines that separate countries, but the prohibitive ones that both society and I placed on myself. In going beyond the borders of a revenue-producing itchy sweater to a big-unknown-wind-in-my-hair-naked-gardening existence, I said yes to showing up. To me. To my life.

In 2017, on my fiftieth birthday, I asked of myself my regrets. There were two. I had a crush on this super-hot guy. We had a lot in common, and I really thought we should date. We'd talked in person at a social gathering once and were friends on social media, so I slid into his DMs (ohmygosh, did I really just say that?). He was polite. I called him out on his George Costanza "it's not you, it's me" line, and felt satisfied that I'd put myself out there. I was also secretly both surprised at and proud of myself for not getting all wrapped up in his *no*. I wanted to find out, so no regret left there.

After serious introspection, I saw I would regret dying having not lived somewhere beautiful. Dallas–Fort Worth wasn't it. You can't really even see beautiful from there. I didn't have a critical illness or anything like that. I turned fifty. A milestone. Miraculous in and of itself. I'd made it through every single decision I'd ever made, hadn't killed myself or anyone else, and if I am to live as long as my Abita, I was literally halfway through my life at that time.

I'd been traveling back and forth to New Mexico for the past nine years and had spent the previous summer in Taos. The Land of Enchantment was truly that for me. Endless turquoise skies, painted deserts, and whispers of those who were gone only in body. It was obvious. So I started telling people Organic conversations that led to perfect renters to occupy (and pay for) my little house. Further communication led me to the rustic cabin of a friend in a health crisis, willing to trade room and board for support. As her crisis eased, an opening to caretake a lovely desert home became available. An offer to occupy a casita during the pandemic showed up just as that caretaking gig ended. Knowing I'd eventually have to pay rent, I worked my ass off delivering groceries during the shutdown. A few personal assistance jobs came from that delivery job, and I fell back into elder care (which I'd done on and off since quitting teaching). With very little overhead, I was able to hoard my hard-earned money and cough up an outrageous deposit to move into a drafty, overpriced, crumbly old adobe.

Living the dream, you say? Indeed, you are correct. When people ask what I do for a living, I say, "I live." Then clarify, "You mean, how do I get money?" I am what I like to call a free agent. Mostly I help people, in all sorts of unconventional ways—not so much from my perspective, but from others looking in at my life. It is not without risk or failure. I show up every day. I drink coffee or I don't. My uniform may be the Emperor's New Clothes, or a hot pink t-shirt and yoga pants. I don't live off a trust fund, alimony, or a cache of lottery money. I still own my little house in Texas, and that's basically my retirement fund. I do have health care, food, an unsold soul, and a full heart. Sometimes I wonder what I've got to show for myself. I wonder about money and if I'll ever find a fulfilling romantic relationship. I wallow there occasionally. When it feels too much, I breathe deep, and give thanks. I remember that the best things in life aren't things. I love and am loved. I have always been provided for. And it's not luck that I live in a drafty, overpriced, crumbly old adobe under enchanted turquoise skies. I am living a self-created life of freedom and smiling, as it is far beyond anything I ever imagined.

Devie Richards • Life Beyond Borders

Devie Richards is a force for good. A life coach and reforestation/planet conservationist, Devie shed her conventional life skin, quit her steady job, and set out to live a life of action and creativity. Whether she's traveling to Honduras to plant trees, leading young adults traveling across India, or at home in Santa Fe painting and making pottery, Devie lives her life by her own authentic design. She's a social justice champion, focusing on human, civil, and women's rights. She is also a writer, photographer, caretaker, daughter, and friend. Devie's coaching approach is primarily focused on empowering others to see what is possible for themselves and to help them realize their dream life *is* actually possible. She encourages her clients to live beyond their borders and discover that they, too, can have a life of meaning, purpose, and pleasure. Follow Devie on:

Instagram (@Butte_tea/ #livebeyondyourborders)
devie.richards@gmail.com.

Misti Wriston

The Day Dude Had to Die *and Other Happy Endings*

Biologically, I have one daughter and three sons—twins and an extremely disabled older son we call Bo. I was also involved in the raising of four stepdaughters, twenty-nine exchange students, and several souls who needed a place for a time.

On the day of this story, one of my boys was driving while the dogs, Bo, and I enjoyed the incredible scenery of Southeast Oklahoma. We were returning from our magical acreage in the forest. The skies were a perfect blue as we drove through the mountains. "Rocket Man" was playing on the radio, and we sang every word while I held Bo's hand. Tears of joy began to fall as I realized that my life, the one I didn't know how I would make it through just two years ago, was perfect. I was overwhelmed with gratitude for being able to live in such a perfect state.

My life was perfect. I had everything. Not everything I could ever think of wanting, of course, and life wasn't without its ups and downs. But I certainly had everything I needed to experience *joy* on a daily basis. This was wealth beyond measure. With tears falling from my eyes, I took a photo of us to remember *this moment of pure joy*.

I let my tears flow, sang with a full voice, and soaked in the unbelievable life I'd created. It was 1:52 p.m. Blessed beyond measure, I was taking deep breaths with overwhelming gratitude and pride as we cruised along.

We got back to my home, and I went to my "Happy Jar." On January 1, 2022, after a Facebook prompt from a dear friend (and author in this very book), I started The Happy Jar. Every time I laughed until I cried, felt joy, felt proud, received a great compliment, saw an amazing bird or view, I wrote the info on a slip of paper. I would take a moment to relive the happy memory in detail before placing it in the jar. I was bottling all the happy in my life into The Happy Jar because (through my work helping others) I *knew* that life would kick me in the proverbial nuts eventually. And when it did, the truth would be that my life is still incredible, regardless of whether a change, a loss, a moment, emotional response, or piece of unpleasant or even tragic news might allow me to think otherwise. I bottled them as a reminder. I let the tears fall again as I remembered every detail of this magical and perfect day, then I added this moment of perfection to The Happy Jar. It was 2:10 p.m.

As my son prepared to return to the city, he told me he needed to say something. I sat. He asked me to define being a victim of abuse.

You know that feeling when your child says something and your brain does an entire circus to find out how to land on both feet and still look like a *mom*? My spidey senses were on high alert. I give my answer in a forced *I-have-my-shit-together-so-no-worries-son* voice. He responded, ever so calmly, "OK, I think we agree."

I mistakenly exhaled and relaxed a smidge. It was 2:15 p.m.

Then he told me…

My ex-husband, his fucking *father*, abused him too. The man who abused me for fifteen years, the man I worked ten years to leave and took two decades to forgive while raising our children alone. The man who has hurt everyone in his path. That man hurt the girls, and now I knew he'd hurt my boys too.

My son told me the abuse he experienced. I listened. We had the most adult conversation imaginable between a twenty-one-year-old man and his fifty-four-year-old mother. I needed grace—from him, the victim! I had done all the counseling and self-help courses for my own familial abuse. But I had nothing for this. No protocol, no words. After thirty-four years and forty children, I had no idea how to parent in that second.

I had no fucking idea how to help, what to say, or how to take the next breath. I knew this part couldn't be about me, no matter what was happening on the inside. I listened. I was thankful to be outside my body as the primal mother in me took over. Our conversation came to a natural conclusion (for that day). We agreed to stop the cycle of silence.

We hugged and exchanged I love you's. I stood outside and watched him drive off, doing the obligatory mom wave until he was no longer visible. My legs began to wobble, my body trembled, heat burned in my eyes, and my throat began to constrict. It felt like I had lost the ability to inhale. I went inside and vomited. I collapsed. Then I cried. It was 3:00 p.m. This was the most a person can handle. I was down. I was done.

Except…I help people who are in this position! I focused on breathing in and out. Somewhere in this human body, I had the information on how to get up. It was there. My tears and crushing emotional pain attempted to trick me into forgetting. I dug deep and could almost feel various parts of my personality arguing. Bo needed me. But the injured momma needed the floor, the tears, and the pain. My imagination wanted to run wild. Misery loves company, and mine was calling for any company it could get. The empowered female, currently buried a lot fucking deeper than normal, knew how to do this. As much as I wanted to lay on the floor and cry until I disappeared, I knew the steps to avoid the quicksand. It was 3:52 p.m. I called the bestie, but she didn't answer. I texted, "Call me, it is mildly urgent." I paced. I cried. I screamed. I vomited. A tiny voice reminded me, "Follow your own advice! Reach out to someone!" I called the male cousin bestie because I knew words must come out, that my imagination was my worst enemy. He answered. I gave the instruction, "I need you to let me talk."

I *spilled*. I said all the things I had never imagined saying to another human in my entire life. Things I had never even considered as a possibility from the vilest person I know. I don't think this happened to "people like us." He listened and let me spew.

Mid-spill, the first bestie beeped in. I switched to her and repeated what is now a part of my life story. It is in pen. It is real. This is not a worry, fear, or movie. This is my family. Depending on if you met me north or south of 2:00 p.m., you met a different woman. This one was changed forever.

Bestie also knew the training. She let me spill. She said I love you. She said she was sorry. She allowed me to discuss, in detail, how I would kill Dude, *their worthless father*, as soon as I found a caregiver for Bo. (Funny how the mind works.) I would kill him that day! This was happening. He was going to die, and it would be painful. She told me she had my back. She said she would drive. Somehow she knew we weren't murdering anyone. She knew I take bees and spiders outside because I don't kill, so she knew. I did not know this yet. To me, this would happen, and at my hand. She knew the words must get out of me, one time, in full.

Then, because she was once the one on the floor and I had lain with her until she could get up, she knew what to do in that moment. She lifted a woman *up*. That is how it works. *You are lifted, you learn, you lift.*

She slowly interjected the smallest amount of humor. She told me she would bring the shovel. Oh my, if you knew her! I pictured her showing up with a flathead screwdriver and her long nails because that is what she uses to dig her plants into the ground. We laughed. She changed my focus for a split second. A tiny crack in the dark, the smallest sliver of light. She asked about my trip out to our perfect land earlier.

Remember two hours ago? Remember *two hours ago* when I was experiencing one of the most joy-filled moments of my life? Remember two hours ago when I was riding in absolute *joy*? Her question about the land I love brought me back, and it clicked. I knew the drill too. I had prepared for this.

Every second is a chance to turn your life around. -Unknown

This was my second, this was my chance.

Nothing was happening at this moment, so my fight-or-flight was not needed. Saving them from the abuse was not an option, so it wasn't worthy of my punishing imagination. I was reacting to my thoughts, emotions, feelings, and memories. We discussed how the children had each had years of therapy to deal with this. I was simply new to this information from the past. I would need to grieve. I would need to remember that this information is not my identity, nor theirs. It is an event that has already occurred. We remembered The Happy Jar. With her on the phone, I reached into The Happy Jar and pulled out my first Therapeutic Happy Slip of the year. I read aloud.

Turn on the song "All the way Up" by Fat Joe, the original version.

This made us both laugh through shared tears. We knew exactly why that slip of paper was in there. We had both happy cried to this recently. The song had reminded us how great our lives were.

She needed to go; it was 4:54 p.m. I put the song on loud and did that thing where you use body movement to improve your emotions. I fake danced until I felt it. At first, I imagine it looked tragic, a fifty-four-year-old woman thrusting and gyrating through tears and snot . . . it helped, though, enough for me to put my training in place. I recalled the way that song reminded me I was about to move *all the way up* a mountain to live in the place dreams are made of. I played it again. And again. I focused on the emotions from *that* memory. I verbally expressed my gratitude for anything and everything I could think of, from the fact that I had friends who helped me out of the dark to the grace my son used to present this horrific information to his mother.

My life is perfect even when it's not. -Ellen DeGeneres

My children are incredible adults. My life was and *is* beautiful. This includes the challenges and pains that life brings. My Happy Jar is surprisingly full so early in the year. On a beautiful Sunday afternoon, I received awful news of a tragedy that happened many years ago. Everyone had had time to process this news except me. There was nothing I could do about it that day. There was nothing I could do to change the facts. I could only support my children through their difficult events ahead and take the time to speak of things aloud, as keeping it inside does unbelievable damage. I could own that my grief was real even while my life, my children, my world, were all still incredible. I could devote time to focus on the act of grieving this, specifically, not as part of a multitasking event. I could devote time alone, on purpose, with the respect I deserved in order to heal. I could read more happy slips from The Happy Jar, watch the sunrise, play with puppies, and love on my friends. I could recall that I am allowed to have pain and joy at the same time, and that I would not feel guilty about that, nor should I! And most importantly, I could be the one who talks about this shit and how to keep going when it hits you. I could be a light to others when a load of darkness slaps them out of nowhere. And I can welcome you back to the light too!

Start a Happy Jar. It might just save another life one day!

Note: No Dudes were harmed in the making of this chapter.

Misti retired as CEO of her insurance and financial services agency at the onset of the pandemic to become sole caregiver for her disabled son in Southeast Oklahoma. She co-owns campgroundtbd and campgroundtbd pantry, providing camping in natural settings, happy animals, and organic food. She also co-owns campgroundtbd publishing, helping authors become published or publish again. A #1 international best-selling author, she mentors those who wish to address addictions, change behaviors or body shape, and improve life by removing their perceived limitations. She believes life is about possibilities and shares her passion for the freedom that comes with love and joy. She can be followed at Barefoot at Heart on Facebook. You can purchase The Happy Jar for yourself at campgroundtbd!

www.facebook.com/labelfreeliving
Barefoot at Heart
www.facebook.com/camptbd
campgroundtbd@gmail.com

Cheryl Roberts Oliver

When Hummingbirds Visit

The Hummingbird is a Native American Symbol of humility, faithfulness, and commitment. *Its vibrant colors symbolize the importance of individuality and its role in nature to pollinate plants. Hummingbird myths depict tiny birds as symbols of the human soul, intelligence, and energy.*

It was early morning September 4, 2012. I was sitting on a white-plastic-patio chair, surrounded by a once pristine xeriscape my brother had created around his house in Arizona. I'd flown to Phoenix from St. Louis the evening before and had gone straight to see my mother at the nursing home.

She couldn't speak, yet the sound she made when she saw me was clear. She knew I was finally there with her. She'd made her choice, refusing to eat after falling and breaking her hip. She gripped my hand, squeezing it, letting me know she had been waiting for me to arrive. I looked in her eyes and told her "It's ok, you can let go now." She sighed and her grip on my hand softened.

I regret that I didn't stay with her all night. I was tired. I wanted a glass of wine and to visit other family members who would be leaving the next day, so I left.

That next morning, beneath Russian Olive and Weeping Willow trees, I was enjoying the lingering coolness that would soon dissipate in the Arizona heat when a hummingbird flew up to me. It hovered near my face for an unusual length of time. I knew my mother was saying goodbye, letting me know her spirit was safe, that she was finally free from the cruel darkness that had trapped her mind, released from her relentless expectations of herself, and that her energy and abilities were vibrant again. The next minute, my sister-in-law came outside and said, "Mom just passed."

Ten years later, at 6:17 this morning, a hummingbird flew into my apartment, hovering from left to right along the east-facing windows, as if searching for the salvia and lavender that I have grown on my balcony for the past twelve years. I acknowledged silently that, "I'm sorry, my life is in transition." Then aloud, "I'm not only not planting flowers. I am pulling up roots." The hummingbird paused, looked at me, then flew out the balcony door.

It sounds quite painful, putting it into words. "Pulling up roots." But that is exactly what is happening to the thirty-five years of my life in St. Louis. I am meticulously and with great respect drawing out, separating and packing my Midwest roots, soon to be transported across Missouri, Kansas, Colorado, up into Wyoming and then down into Utah near the now seriously evaporated Great Salt Lake. That is where I will build a new nest, this time on the fourteenth floor of an urban cliff dwelling, again with a balcony facing east, this time with a view up Emigration Canyon where scrub oak, sage and rabbit brush cover the steep foothills. I will observe their changing colors during each of the four seasons in Salt Lake City, and no doubt, photographically document sunrises, storm clouds, full moons and winter fog. It's what I do.

When asked, I tell people I'm moving back to my original habitat- the arid, higher elevations of the intermountain west. This is a deliberate choice. My daughter and I want to live closer to each other, to share what remains of my life and the next wonderful phases of her life. We are creating time and space for our ancient spirits to coalesce, courageously bridging from one to the other, often invisible, side.

I remember my transition in July 1987, having just moved to St. Louis from Salt Lake City. It was not what I expected. Five months after I moved, I turned forty and knew the next phase would require a total do-over.

Sara was five. Our favorite thing was to go for drives, picnics and hikes into the state parks and recreational areas, looking for our connection in nature. We would get in the car, and after buckling up, Sara would ask, "Where are we getting lost today, Mommy?"

I always replied, "Let's find out." It didn't matter that I didn't have an answer. Answers weren't as relevant as the questions in those early days in the Midwest. (It's still true, even now.) Our story was about discovery and rediscovery, each transition alternately closing and opening doors in our lives. We transmuted our need for ritual and tradition by celebrating the cycles of the earth: the Spring and Autumnal Equinoxes, the Winter and Summer Solstices. The rituals we created allowed us to both honor the separation from what we'd known and consciously act to form a new way of being.

We moved five times before Sara graduated from high school in 2000, from unincorporated St. Louis to a residence (or two) in the Clayton School District. With other scholarship offers on the table, Sara chose to return to Salt Lake City to attend the University of Utah, my alma mater, and be closer to her dad, who had moved back a few years after we divorced in 1986.

After Sara moved to Utah to go to the university, I moved another four times, all around the city, from Clayton to the Central West End, then University City, finally returning to the city limits bordering the edge of Clayton. Those were tumultuous years, fueled by alcohol, depression and a codependent second marriage. It's clear looking back, but boy, was it ever muddled while living it.

Muddled may be a perfect word–saying it aloud sounds its meaning. The only way I know to emerge after being pulverized is to completely let go of whatever was anticipated, submitting to the essence that is released. *One must never rush the process when a substance breaks down into a simpler substance.*

Attempting to find my way out of acute *muddlement*, I divorced my second husband and moved into my urban cliff dwelling in 2010; retired from an eleven-year executive director position in 2018; gave up alcohol in 2019; turned back into an introvert during the pandemic; and now, in 2022, I prepare to abandon the innumerable shades of green and winding brown rivers of this region. Seeking simplicity and striving for cogent authenticity, I am ready to return to the mountains and deserts of the west.

When the hummingbird visited me just after sunrise on this nineteenth day of June, stirring the unusually cool air, its emerald feathers flashing in the brilliant sunlight, I thought of those who are no longer here: Mom and Dad, Sara's father, oldest brother, friends and partners from former lives. I thought about the coming Summer Solstice–the longest day and only passage to the longest night. I've observed the moon and sun, the stars and planets and learned that answers dwell most often in the darkness, waiting to be emancipated by timely, meaningful questions and honest, deliberate actions.

I moved here in July. I'm moving back in July. You'd think I'd have learned what not to do after the first time, since July is *the* hottest month in both cities. Not ideal. Symbolic? Heat that purifies? Perhaps. I'm just grateful Sara and her boyfriend will be with me for this journey, driving the U-Haul, me following in the Kia Niro with Ava and Stella, my aging dachshunds. I am fearful, but I won't be alone. That's the fundamental reason I am moving: to be nearer to Sara; to keep living independently but be within reach of family; continue my late-stage career as writing coach/creative editor; and make new friendships while nurturing some of those I am leaving behind. I realize only a few will be sustained, no matter how important they seem now. Just like many of the people I was close to before I retired, only a few kept in touch, and I'm not on Facebook enough to track the lives that others post.

Yes, there is an emptiness. Or could it be an opening? A lightness. I am shedding what was and may have been to create the final phase of my life for as long as I am mentally and physically able. It is precarious. I am, after all, turning seventy-five in November. By that time, I hope to be fully settled in my new nest, greeting Mother Sun rising over a snow-covered canyon instead of an urban park. Sara and I will celebrate the Winter Solstice with those we love. I will have sought out new opportunities, found people with whom I share common interests, and taken an even deeper dive into my poetry.

From this pre-move vantage point, I envision myself being safe, healthy, vibrant and creative, full of laughter and empathy, loving and being loved. My dogs and I will walk in the mornings and afternoons for as long as we are able. I will say yes to short hikes next to a mountain stream, or a long walk along the foothills. Which, oddly enough, brings me back to this moment in time. I think I'll take another walk in Forest Park and later, I'll purchases a few salvia and place them in the planter boxes on the balcony, to share their blooms with the visiting hummingbird for another twenty-eight days. Purple, I think. Yes, I will get purple salvia to nourish my spirit as I box up my life and say my goodbyes.

Cheryl Roberts Oliver is lead writing coach and creative editor for Davis Creative Publishing Partners, and a poet. Her master's and bachelor's degrees in English literature and creative writing were the foundation for every position she held during more than seven different careers. Her professional life was formed in layers as she sought out increasing levels of responsibility working in advertising and public relations, transition management, corporate marketing, executive development, adjunct faculty at two universities, and culminating in her role as executive director for two nonprofit organizations over twenty-two years. Her best advice: start writing, then keep writing. Sharing stories is our best chance for thriving, as is walking through a misty forest, along a stream, or into the early morning desert after a rainstorm.

www.facebook.com/cheryl.oliver.948

The Afterword

Thank you for reading *Here Comes the Sun: Step Up, Shine Your Light, Share Your Brilliance!* I am humbled by the women who accepted our invitation to contribute and by the amount of love we have experienced in this creative process. I am a better me because of the relationships formed in this process. It is my hope that you were able to receive this love as well, from one of us or from many.

The words in this book have changed who I am as a Woman. The experience of an anthology of this nature is hard to express, even for authors. I am a better woman for my work in *Here Comes the Sun*. I am a better human because of the power of the words in this book. Words are incredibly powerful—spoken, read, and written. I have written many words in my life. Teachers made me write "I will not talk in class." The punishment didn't stop me from sharing my light, and somehow it opened the door to writing all kinds of things:

- Letters to lovers back when we wrote and mailed them.
- Countless diaries and journals, poems, and fairy tales.
- Lists I followed and more that never made it to the store.
- Letters to make amends when it was not safe to do so in person.
- Letters that had the last word, some never meant to send, and some meant to hurt.

- Letters to some who passed on before I could say my words, which were later burned.
- Emails, blogs, texts.
- Endless books and chapters started and discarded.

In this book, I created an opportunity to write a letter to my unborn grandchild: #IamHoney. I was also able to see my daughter published for the first time. These are gifts!

For the past thirty years, the number and quality of our written interactions have diminished. What used to be long, heartfelt, hand-penned letters are now *wyd?* and *ttyl*. We have lost access to the art of language, the growth and escape it provides. Growing older and wiser, I have identified that writing is my therapy, even—or perhaps especially—when the words were never meant for others to read. Writing is my release, my path to find clarity. I found healing in my writing. And finally, writing and publishing created a way to share this amazing space.

My calling is to be of service to others, so I will follow my natural inclination and share the therapeutic process I find in writing and in nature. I offer four simple steps that have helped me even when I did not think I wanted to be helped. If these steps can also take you outside, surrounded by nature, even better! I find a walk in the woods erases a lot of my writer's block or, at the very least, makes it less important for a time.

The Steps

Step One: Spill the words in your head onto paper or a computer. Whatever you are thinking about, write it down. It can be your grocery list, your to-do list, a favorite poem or scripture, lyrics to a song, what your neighbor did that irked you—just dump it all out! Like me, you may find all the words dancing in your imagination, and the thoughts that are held captive, maddening. Step one, spill! If you draw a blank, write about anyone or anything that makes you feel grateful! Keep the words flowing. This will also help your brain "think" differently by allowing access to vocabulary you haven't used in a while. Stir up those sleepy creative neurons. Find synonyms for the words you really want, wish, desire, or crave to express. Finally, even if all you've written down is the grocery list, jazz it up with your delicious, mouth-watering words.

Step Two: Release your frustration. When you are ready, write one thing that is bothering or confusing you: a struggle, a goal, a dream, a wish. Start with generalities and then get specific. If possible, stay present with a single topic; explore the facts and emotions surrounding it and pay attention to how they are interacting. If you get sidetracked, come back to your topic. Then, when you are ready, stop writing and rest.

Step Three: Rewrite the story with *your* ending. Make it exactly as you desire it to be! Get specific about what it looks like, smells like, feels like in this new version. Write as many endings as you can think of! Add comedy and use words that make the story hilarious. Write science fiction, romance, poetry.

Step Four: Repeat as needed. The goal is not to end up with perfectly written or even legible pages. The goal is to purge a bit of the extra noise you carry around in your mind, to invite clarity and peace to enter into your real-life story and ignite that little light in your head so it can shine unfiltered, unfettered. You and your brain can untangle a lot of issues once that noise settles down.

This is how writing helps me. I hope you will allow it to help you as well. I have an incredible editor and writing coach, Cheryl Roberts Oliver. I am not a writing coach. I am a woman who coaches people to *Live, Love*

Nature, and To Write. I help publish those that are ready for the challenge, either electronically or in person on our magical mountain top in Southeast Oklahoma. Write where you are or come write with us! I am at a beautiful place where my passion, purpose, and profession intersect. I hope that by reading the amazing stories and hearing the voices featured in this book, you will find your own words falling onto paper.

With love,
Misti

campgroundtbd@gmail.com
campgroundtbdpublishing.com
www.facebook.com/camptbd
www.facebook.com/MistiWriston
#IamHoney